THE MORE THINGS CHANGE

A Reflection of a Journey from 1947 to 2008

H. L. Whitlock

THE MORE THINGS CHANGE

A Reflection of a Journey from 1947 to 2008

H. L. Whitlock

MILLIGAN BOOKS,INC.   BOOKS   CALIFORNIA

Printed and Bound in the United States of America
Published and Distributed by:
Milligan Books

Cover Design K Borne
Formatting: Milligan Books

First Printing, July 2008
10 9 8 7 6 5 4 3 2 1

ISBN 978-0-9815783-4-7

Library of Congress Cataloging-in-Publication Data
H.L. Whitlock,
 The More Things Change
 p. cm.

Milligan Books, Inc.
1425 W. Manchester Ave., Suite C
Los Angeles, California 90047
www.milliganbooks.com
drrosie@aol.com
(323) 750-3592

Dedication

I dedicate this book to my parents and my siblings, without them, this book would not exist. Moreover, I thank and praise God for my parents and family. Without God, there is no life. I acknowledge His grace and goodness and boldly declare His hand-prints are smeared all over goodness.

Contents

From left to right: Dot, The Kid, Ethel, Sally, Book. Seated: Fannie, Pete.

From left to right: Fannie and Haymon

Pete

Introduction

As I PEERED DOWN THE corridors of my mind, I recall beginning this story you're about to read years ago. I had told my family and friends about the project, but would get stuck in the miry clay of stagnation and procrastination. Probably one of my biggest and most glaring faults is my lack of punctuality accompanied with procrastination.

Many years ago, I agreed to take a friend to LAX after he had told me the time his flight was departing and the time I should be at his residence. Unfortunately, I reached his residence at a time making it impossible for him to catch his flight. Yes, he missed it. After that, if he wanted me to do something important at a particular time, he'd tell me to come an hour or two earlier than the actual time he wanted me there.

I felt awful for a long time because I had caused him to miss his flight, and I did try to work on that aspect of my behavior. Once, someone accused me of being un-American because I was always tardy. Another person claimed that it was an example of "colored folks' time."

I recall arriving at my church, Mt. Tabor Missionary Baptist Church, extremely late one Sunday morning with the pastor half finished preaching. I sat in the narthex and listened to the conclusion of his sermon. As I did so, I scribbled the following on a sheet of paper taken from a table: "A person who continues to be late for that which is scheduled is disorganized and has a problem." A psychologist stated, "A person with a recognizable problem is more apt to deal with it than one who has an unrecognizable problem."

To-date, I am still working on correcting my tardiness flaw.

Most importantly, I'm somewhat piqued Mother has expired without having read my narration. Ironically, during her hospitalization, a publishing company wanted to publish my memoirs, but I just couldn't bring my focus together due to Mother's illness.

One thought she kept pounding in the heads of her six children was, "You all stick together and be there for each other; and be there for your children and your children's children." In all honesty, we have always adhered to that good advice. Ethel, my oldest sister, said just recently, "We're all still here, thanks to God, we six little eggs."

Whenever anything bad affected our family, Ethel, even at the tender age of five or six, would go underneath the house and pray. Having firsthand knowledge of the things for which she prayed, Jesus, no doubt, interceded with the Father and answered her prayers. All my sisters are kindhearted, God-fearing servants to the indigent and the sick, but they can't compare to Ethel. To say she is overly engaging would be an understatement. She's so radiant, her character absolutely glows.

She knew as a child she would become a teacher one day, because she is naturally gifted in that area.

Dot, my sister next to Ethel, is disabled after having worked many years. God gives everyone certain talents. God gave Dot talent in the area of art, decorating, fashion, and cooking. I recall she drew a mural-like picture of a metropolitan scene depicting buildings, streets, streetlights, etc. She watched mother and became her understudy at cooking and is known by our siblings as the "Black Martha Stewart." To-date, we still host Christmas dinners at Dot's. *Superb* is an understatement for what she can put on the dinner table. About two Christmases ago, I couldn't stop going back for refills, and after I finished eating, I offered to help wash dishes. Dot's husband bantered, "No! Sit your behind down before you work up *another* appetite." Laughter filled the entire room.

Sally is the youngest sister who is an RN and does administrative tasks at Grady's Hospital. It's the biggest trauma center in Atlanta, Georgia. Not only is she a good nurse, she has also expanded her writing skills and writes appeals. She's been very successful in recovering large amounts of money for the hospital.

The Kid, the elder of the three brothers, retired from General Motors in 1996, in Doraville, Georgia. He has been my mentor ever since I can recall. He once declared, "I'm going to get a Volkswagen," and that produced laughter and scorn by those listening while shooting basketball. But, after getting his Volkswagen around 1962, his friends started buying Volkswagens, including a neighbor, a young man who lived just a few houses from us.

The Kid was the first family member to buy land and eventually build his house, an early American-styled home built in 1968 in Atlanta. He was so proud whenever he made payments on his land. One day he went in to make a payment and the person to whom he spoke asked, "How much are you paying today?" He exclaimed, "I'm paying *everything*."

The Kid's greatest asset is his common sense, a trait which I thrived on for much of my life. I always appreciate his advice.

Buck, the youngest of the siblings, shortly after finishing high school, took a one-year hiatus and got a job at a paint company. At that time, it was on the same street on which we lived. I was working at General Motors making decent money during that time. Buck would walk toward our house with paint smeared on his pants and shirt, and I would joke, "Here comes ole big money." He displayed a smirk, and I a smile. His salary was really meager.

Buck boldly proclaimed to a co-worker that he could draw a machine that was inside the paint company. This machine was a large paint-mixing one with either a vortex or cylindrical feature. The co-worker just chuckled in disbelief.

Ironically, that same evening, Buck phoned Dekalb Tech to enroll in drafting and, fortunately, they had an opening.

While he was in high school, Buck excelled in mechanical drawing. His teachers and classmates called him a wizard. Buck's proudest moment came when his art work was on display along with projects from other students representing the entire county of Dekalb. At the symposium, then-governor and segregationist Lester Maddox acknowledged the winner of the most elite projects and presented medals to them. First prize went to a White male student. Buck won runner-up, winning second prize. Many people whispered that Buck should have won first place.

After his education, Buck worked for Mr. John Portman, whose work figured in the DuPont Mansion. Additionally, he's credited with working on the Bonaventura Hotel in Los Angeles, the Twin Towers in New York, the Atlanta Fulton County Jail, and many of the buildings in the metropolitan area of Atlanta. During the 1996 Olympics, he had the privilege of drawing the soccer field for the games.

Buck eventually began to design clothes. As a child, he was always very talented. He has been highly recognized and honored, appearing twice in the *Atlanta Journal and Constitution*. He is probably one of the best dressed men who have ever lived.

Haymon, our father, sacrificed his time for us. He loved his job. He worked 33 years at the Pullman Company, which relocated first to St. Louis, and then eventually to Chicago. He was gone a lot, but his separation from us gave us the means to thrive and prosper.

Our mother, Fannie, worked for these three White ladies who were sisters, doing household chores. Our entire family is so thankful to our parents, who made it possible for us to complete our education and succeed in life.

CHAPTER
One

Growing Up In the South

Growing up in the suburban section of Atlanta, Georgia, he could still hear his mother's voice echoing in his ears, "Pete, you better do your work around the house first before going into those woods hunting, looking up in a bird's behind." As a child, hunting was akin to religion, a way of life. His slingshot, which they called a 'flip', was lethal and an unfair advantage to birds, rabbits, squirrels, snakes and lizards. Pete shot it with remarkable accuracy.

The community in which Pete lived was Washington Park, Decatur, Georgia. Of the hundred and fifty-nine counties in Georgia, Decatur is located in Dekalb County, adjacent county to Atlanta, Fulton County. Of course, Fulton County is the great county where Dr. Martin Luther King, Jr. was reared and not to mention where the epic movie "Gone With The Wind" debuted.

Washington Park was known for its cemetery and meadows. Kraft Foods complex was on the property of Mr. Scott, who leased out to Kraft, and presently has a Krogers store and surrounding stores that replaced the Kraft Foods

1

complex. He was very slight in stature with a weird, foreboding appearance. Since Mr. Scott's death, his son has become the heir to a tremendous spread of land. But his father, by the observation of many, Mr. Scott was considered a miser.

Directly in front of Pete's house across the street, one could see Mr. Scott on this very old-looking tractor in the wheat field with its bush-cutting arm hewing the wheat. Buck, Pete's younger brother, has always been small for his age. On one hot summer day, he took Mr. Scott a big glass of ice-water. What nerves and fortitude! Buck probably performed the magnanimous gesture to acquire money from him, but received only a thank-you.

Pete remembered when Washington Park had dirt roads and vividly the era in which his older brother, Kid, sisters Ethel and Dot dated. They would have lawn parties and house get-togethers. Benny, who lives near the community, converted a moderate size house into a Juke-Joint. The wooden floors with the friction of shoe heels and soles gave off reverberation sounds. The house had a juke-box, and comprised classic hits such as "Your Precious Love," by Jerry Butler, "Heat Wave," by Martha Reeve and The Vandellas, "Hitch Hike," by Marvin Gaye, "Do You Love Me," by The Contours. Pete recalls clearly Junior Broad, who would get into a corner, crossing his arms and hands caressing his back as if he were osculating a female. The Contours song would pause and the bass would do his number, and Junior Broad would mimic the bass. Junior Broad once sang in the church choir at Greater Friendship Baptist Church. While visiting the church, Pete confided after reminding him of his antics at the sing-along, "At that point back then, I knew you could sing," eliciting a broad smile and light laughter from Junior.

Pete has always admired his oldest brother, Kid, and recalls his first automobile, a nineteen-fifty Oldsmobile coupe.

The jet-black auto had been drenched with several coats of paint.

On one occasion while at a date's house, the damsel's father remarked, "What did you do to that car to make it shine like that?"

"I kinda dusted it off," replied Kid.

"Uh,uh, you scrubbed that thang," exclaimed the father of his date.

When Pete entered the 8th grade, Kid had graduated the previous year, and some of the girls who dated and liked Kid would inquire, "Aren't you Kid's little brother?"

"Yes," he confirmed.

Margrette, a very attractive fair complexion girl with huge eyes from Washington Park, was Kid's steady girlfriend, whom he married shortly after graduating from high school, a marriage to-date, exceeding over 40 years. Most afternoons when school ended, he would park across the street from Hamilton High in a spacious lot near the store, and would pick her up there.

Pete, meanwhile, enjoyed his free time hunting. Drawing a comparison to Pete's slingshot, aka, 'flip' skills, the mind evokes King David of the Bible. King David was known for his slingshot skills and performed it with amazing feats. He faced unenviable odds and was pitted against Goliath of Gath, who was a giant. Biblical accounts describe his height six cubits and a span. During ancient times the measure of length regarding a cubit, was approximately 18 to 22 inches. A span, in measurement, is the distance between the tip of a man's thumb and the tip of his middle finger when the hand is spread out—about 9 inches.

In essence, Goliath in height was approximately 141 inches. That's roughly the equivalent of two 6 feet men, 144 inches. His combat ware was even more astonishing, featuring a helmet of brass, armed with a coat of mail, weighed down with five thousand shekels of brass; with greaves of brass on his legs, and a target of brass between his shoulders. He possessed a spear-like weaver beam, with the spear's head weighing six hundred shekels of iron, plus a shield to protect his body.

Conversely, David's armor was initially designated by Saul, who girded him with a helmet of brass and a coat of mail, and given a sword and armor. However, David removed them, took his staff in hand, and chose five smooth stones out of a brook, placing them in a shepherd's bag and took his slingshot with him to confront his foe.

Similar to Pete, David loved the Lord and trusted Him. Saul expressed pessimism to David about going up against a man who had practiced combat since his youth—where David was a youth and inexperienced. David, however, narrated to Saul that once upon a time, he, then a servant, kept his father's flock. This lion and bear came and took a lamb from the flock, seeking and finding the predators; he struck it and freed the lamb from its mouth.

Once the predator rose up against him, he grabbed its beard and slew it, killing both the lion and the bear.

David was quick to acknowledge the Lord delivered him from those predators, and assured Saul the Lord would do likewise when facing the Philistine.

Upon approaching Goliath, he took a stone from his bag with slingshot in hand and slew him. Henceforth, his prestige soared to unprecedented heights.

Many times Pete would venture into the woods hunting before doing chores around the house and upon returning home, his mother, Fannie, would meet him with a thick leather strap, very similar to those used in a barber shop. She loved him dearly but didn't spare the rod. Never did she hit him in the face, always the buttocks, back and legs. What contemporary society observes as child abuse in the past, empiricism construes it justifiable chastisement and a necessary punishment.

4

Pete, like many adolescents, possessed the proclivity to wildness and whimsicalness, though x-raying his heart, he wasn't a bad person. His idiosyncrasy mirrored what his mother and father taught him, including "Do unto others as you would have them do unto you, don't take what isn't yours, respect your elders, attend church and always love and believe in and trust God, etc."

Pete really loved his elders and would naturally aid the need of them. While hunting, he and his brother, Buck, would go through the cemetery and would see Mr. Wallace digging a grave with a pick and shovel. And for a medium size boy, Pete was very strong with tremendous stamina. Sympathy and concern drew Pete to the grave and he would help his friend, and didn't resume hunting until the grave was completely dug. At that time, a grave had to be six feet deep which was slightly over Pete's height of 5-feet 10 inches. As always, Mr. Wallace would give Buck money to fetch Top Colas. During the late 50s and early 60s, the proprietor of the cemetery didn't own a backhole digger which meant the graves had to be dug manually. Mr. Wallace was dark complexion, who was about 5 feet 9 and walked slue-footed. He was handsomeless, but forthrightness and integrity shone very brightly.

Pete heralded from a middle class Black-American family, consisting of three sisters and three brothers including himself. Since his father worked in a different state for many years, his mother was forced into a single parent role. Fannie was a strong Christian lady, extremely pretty, fair complexion with natural black and straight-like hair. She set lofty goals for her children, insisting that each finish school and stay into the academic network of learning. After completing the first grade, she had to drop out of school to work to support her family. Born August 24, 1924, she had firsthand experience of tough times, the fall of the stock market, coupled with economic woes.

In spite of her poor educational background, she instilled in all six of her children to complete school and press further. Contrary to her poor education, she was a bright, no-nonsense achiever, and if one didn't know her educational level; when discovering her short school tenure one would be surprised by the way she presented herself, no one would have thought that she had such little education. Therefore people shouldn't be too quick to assume another's level of intelligence by their speech. In fact, a shiny speech does not denote a bright mind, and conversely, a not-so-handsome vocabulary, in many cases may have an iron-clad mind of brilliance. Confirmation of being an achiever mirrors the achievements meted in the lives of her children.

The oldest son, Kid, after completing high school, went on to become a career General Motors employee who retired Dec. 20, 1996. Next in age is Ethel, who attended Savannah State College and is a school-teacher; next is Dot, who has become a career employee at an insurance company, but became disabled due to a back injury; Pete, subsequently to completing high school, became employed at Sears, as a salesman/receiving clerk and shortly following became employed at General Motors. Since those stints, completed a course in Telecommunications; performed office work and telecommunications duties, and has become self-employed in an upholstery/carpet cleaning service.

Sally, who is thirteen months younger, attended college and majored in nursing, and afterward, became an R.N., she now works at one of the biggest trauma centers in Atlanta, Georgia, doing administrative tasks. Her adept technical writing skills, saves the company an obscene amount of money.

Lastly, Buck, the youngest of all her children, after finishing basic education, attended a tech-college and majored in drafting. During high school, he was an astute draftsman and nothing short of a marvel at his craft. Astonishingly, during his senior year of high school a symposium was in place showcasing the most elite drafting projects of students from all counties of Georgia, and ironically, Buck came in second place although word was, he should have come in first place. Buck was proud still to be recognized and honored. The then Governor Lester Maddox, bestowed upon him a plaque.

Buck worked many years at an engineering firm in the Atlanta area as a designer/draftsman, who's credits are traced to many of the erected buildings in the Atlanta area; namely the Fulton County Jail. He's also credited to the soccer field on which the Olympians played in 1996. Amazingly, he's also credited with work done on the befallen twin towers in New York during their construction.

Meanwhile, Pete's best friend was John, who too lived in Washington Park. Around the age of five, one of Pete's associates, Sammy, encouraged Pete to fight John. "Hit him," exclaimed Sammy. Pete, though very strong and capable, never liked fighting, but the diabolical Sammy kept insisting, "Hit him, hit him." An inswelling of pity overcame Pete, who said "No! He ain't done nothing to me." John was a nice and easy guy who didn't bother anyone. From that point on, they became closest of friends, a friendship that never ended. Pete really loved John.

John was a guy with excellent intelligence. He accomplished much of what he aspired to do.

Pete and John were the same age, and during the tenth grade, they struggled with their shorthand class. John, who is very fair complexion and a rather handsome young man, he went to this book store to try to acquire the same shorthand book with translation as Miss Alice, their teacher had. After describing himself as an educator, his charisma and demeanor got the job done. When Alice asked Pete to read that day's assignment, he did so with fluidity. She immediately demanded, "Pete, bring me that book." Yes, he was busted, bringing laughter from fellow students.

A similar occasion arose during their ninth school year, while most of the classmates in history class were poised to flunk a pending test, within hours, Pete was privy to a copy of the test, giving it to Ethel's (his sister) boyfriend, Tommy. He was smart as they came. After filling out the blank test, Pete shared it with John and Ann, a friend who lived three houses from Pete. Their history teacher, Mr. Chattum, was a robust Black-American man with a very dark complexion, who, upon sight, struck fear into the hearts of every schoolchild.

"All right, remove everything from the top of your desk," he instructed. After giving the test, he revealed the scores, and of the entire class of around thirty students, only four passed. The smartest student in the class, Mary Hall, scored 72. Ann scored 99½. Mr. Chattum shared Ann's score and kept uttering "Ninety-nine and a half, almost perfect...Almost perfect." While revealing John and Pete's scores, he said, "John, guessed his way to 81½...And Pete, 82½." This brought humor and laughter from fellow students.

These instances were the only two that John and Pete cheated on tests throughout their school tenure. If ever there was a time when Pete didn't apply himself to his highest potential, it was during school. Had he done so, he would have certainly made higher grades, instead, he barely made passing grades. Of all the teachers Pete encountered, Mr. Steward, his biology teacher was deemed the smartest, even John echos this perspective to-date. How smart was he? He certainly knew Pete day-dreamed and paid little to no attention to what was taught. Just prior to having a test he advised everyone to place their notes and books into the base of their desks. "Pete, you may leave yours and anything else atop your desk." Fellow classmates chuckled. There were additional chuckles during the test's aftermath when Mr. Steward revealed each score of the students, particularly Pete's score. It was the lowest. Mr. Steward knew Pete didn't take serious notes or pay serious attention. Any solace to Pete's mind was that many of his classmates flunked the exam. A note was given to Pete for his parents to come see Mr. Steward. The teacher apprised that he would remove everyone's failed scores if he or she improves on the next exam. Meanwhile, Fannie visited the teacher and learned that Pete wasn't attentive in class and needed to improve. Deep down, it bothered him to see his mother having to visit the teacher for something he could avoid. He self-resolved to do better and to never have his mother visit any teacher due to low grades. True to himself, he worked hard and improved his grades in Biology. In fact, Mr. Steward removed the failed score from the previous exam.

Pete's favorite subject was English and his favorite teacher was Mrs. Brown, who taught English. Though timid and quiet, many of his classmates presumably deemed him not so smart. Realistically, he was average and made sub-standard grades. The quintessential perspectives to doing well in school are: Paying attention, reading and studying during extra times...unfortunately, none of these belonged to Pete on a consistent basis. Although he was quiet, he learned and absorbed more in English than any other subject.

Mrs. Brown was a smart teacher who displayed a lot of humor, so much humor until Pete was taciturn much of the time. Example, a classmate would say, "Mrs. Brown, may I be excused, I don't feel well and want to go lay down?" "Lay down, you might hatch an egg, you mean lie down." Laughter from fellow classmates ensued. She would ask a student to read, "I'm fit'na," replied the student. "Fit'na," exclaimed Mrs. Brown. "Come write fit'na on the blackboard, if anything, you're going to correct your grammar," she advised. Ebonics was definitely in effect there. Once a classmate uttered, "I'mo do it. "I'mo, write that also on the board." Correct grammar would be, I am going, Mrs. Brown informed.

One particular day, she asked this student to read...This young man began reading slowly, and when he got to an unfamiliar word, he'd say "big word" and continued reading. Mrs. Brown would say, "Go back to that word and let's break it down into syllables." After learning how to enunciate the word, he'd continue reading in a noticeably slow, stumbling and babbling way until at one point he lamented, "Damn." Mrs. Brown would comment, "His reading was so pathetic and frustrating until he uttered that sigh." Laughter permeated the entire classroom.

Shortly after completing high school, John attended tech-college and took a trade in repairing typewriters, cash registers, adding machines, etc. Pete was slated to attend tech-college as well. His mother, Fannie, refused to sign for him to get a 1966 Chevelle Super Sport, and this infuriated him. So he deferred schooling and instead, took his 1954 Ford Customline and converted it into a classic. His brother, Kid, coordinated the plot pertaining to its gold color and general appearance. From inside, featuring white roll'in pleats seats and sidings; white overhead leather lining; gold carpet on the floors, with the base of the doors and general base trimmed in gold carpet, and a white racing steering wheel; featuring Firestone racing tires and American-Aluminum mag wheels. The coil springs installed on the front were intended and designed for a 454 Mercury engine. Heavy duty shocks were installed on front to help absorb bumpiness. The rear had air shocks. The entire car was slightly elevated, providing a suave and savvy appearance. John was credited to having rebuilt the engine, a 390. He replaced some of its contents with oversize parts. He had an uncanny knack at disassembling and reassembling objects. Kid, after seeing the engine torn down to a short block remarked, "If you can put all that back together in working order, you are a good one." John had the heads shaved, changed the lifts from hydrologic to solid 427 valve springs; had a specially made cam (street and strip reed racing cam); personally rebuilt the three-two-barrel carburetors. He would later confirm with a smile, "You know, I've never done this before, I watched someone else and learned."

The car was renowned and legendary for its appearance. The girls went wild over it, some would follow Pete and would ask to be taken for a ride. Some, enthusiasm would subdue emotion and lead them to the car, and occasionally Pete would return from a convenient store and find a woman sitting in it. The automobile was nothing short of a classic, and became a conversation-piece and would be mentioned in conversations for over thirty years later.

John had a 1955 Ford with a 390 engine also. To-date, Pete never knew all the details of his engine, but learned the heads were shaved to sixty thousands compared to Pete's thirty thousands. John's auto had awesome power, and when idling, similarly to a pianist pressing keys, generating harmonious sounds, some individuals would say it sounded like a band with unique notes. One day John took Buck and Pete for a ride on the main street, John came to a complete stop, placing the three-speed transmission into first gear, revved it to high rate of speed and depressed the accelerator. Similarly to the take-off of a 747 Jet, the force of the engine thrust their backs against the seats with tremendous pressure as the car's front rose as if the car was about to ascend; simultaneously, the rear wheel spun throughout the complete ratio of first and second gears for about 80 feet on the asphalt street. After coming out of second gear, he spent the balance of the time breaking down its speed in an attempt to bring the auto to a stop.

Buck and Pete acknowledged John's car possessed more power than any car in which they had ridden. It really had jet-like speed.

John's car was light and medium green, that two-tone car was also very beautiful. Kid dubbed it the "Creeper." Once upon a time when the community had dirt roads and John had moved from the community, the car was driven so slowly with the musical engine doing repeated encore, leading Kid to come up with "Creeper." Usually when driving it near the city area stores in Decatur, GA, one could see him glancing and staring at his reflection in store windows as if he were window shopping. Rather, he was simply admiring his car.

Admittedly, he was most proud having rebuilt the engine in Pete's car. Pete would very seldom drag-race. Kid advised Pete to never drag-race. He told Pete that if someone says to you, "Lets race," just say, "I have a show-caser, not a racer." However, on one occasion, a guy kept insisting, "Come on, let go...Are you afraid?" Unfortunately, on one rainy evening, Pete had had a flat tire. The car had four Firestone racing tires. One of the rear tires was replaced with a regular or conventional rim and tire which spun out while he was drag-racing. When word got back to John what had happened, he was infuriated, "You know better than that, using a spare tire drag-racing in the rain, that's stupid."

T<small>CHAPTER</small>wo

The Establishment of a Relationship

URING THE FALL OF 1967, Pete's life would take a twist like never before after he met Sonia, a White girl who had recently moved from South Georgia and lived then on the same street as he. For weeks, the young lady in the blue-gray 1962 Chevrolet would stare and smile at Pete. And once they ended up at a convenient store at the same time. It gave him an up-close-and-personal look at the petite, huge brown eyed brunette. Being shy, he had a melt-down once they were face to face. He gave her a reciprocal smile and quickly turned his head in utter shyness. Years later, she commented on that particular occasion, "I looked at you and thought you were gonna die," she said.

At that time she lived with her mother, step-father and sister and occasionally her step-father's son would visit the family. Pete resided in a Black-American community. The main street where he lived, the north side was occupied by Whites. He lived a quarter of a mile from their two-bedroom apartment.

Heading south on the main two-way street on a lovely Sunday evening, Pete was to see a reluctant date. Traveling northbound was Sonia and as both cars came to a stop. "What going on?" He asked.

"Nothing, where are you on your way to?" She inquired.

"Maybe to a movie," he replied.

After exchanging names, he requested to meet her the next evening to get better acquainted. She agreed. These short meetings took place each evening that particular week until he suggested they meet at the north Dekalb Mall, and for her to follow him to his uncle's place just off Montreal Rd. An evening spearheading what seemingly was the start of the beginning of the rest of their lives. Unalike attraction could have been the curiosity that brought them together, but love and an unmatched drive and strong reciprocity made their relationship inseparable. Despite the prejudice and hatred targeted towards Blacks from Whites, such dating was dangerous and risky business.

Even Peggy Lipton, one of the star actors in Mod Squad, went on record describing when she and Quincy Jones were married, and visiting her southern hometown, he had to get down in the car to avoid being stopped or who knows what would happen.

In 1968, Pete suffered a severe strain and eventually had to be hospitalized. Sonia obviously wanted to see him prior to, during, and after hospitalization. At first, his family was reluctant to allowing such visitation. Their reluctance wasn't born out of prejudice, rather, protection and safety of their home. Yet, Pete's kind-hearted family allowed her to visit. She and Fannie exchanged greetings as they sat down together to discuss matters. Overall, Fannie liked her but did register concerns regarding their safety and well-being. Sonia had a large get-well card in hand for Pete where she disclosed, "I love him."

Fannie said to Sonia, "It isn't wrong to fall in love with someone, it's just that, I fear the harm others could cause you and my son." And further asserted, "Some White people would rather see you two dead than alive together...you must be careful," related Fannie.

"I understand, we will be careful," she assured.

Perhaps it was curiosity that brought them together, but it was the bond of love that made them inseparable. Ironically, initially after meeting and seeing each other, they didn't miss a day seeing one another for about three months. Prior to their courtship, Pete had befriended a young lady from Greenville, GA, about 70 miles south of Atlanta, Georgia. At the time, she was in the Job Corps, Omaha, Nebraska. Pete liked her, but couldn't see himself settling down with her. Inwardly while driving from Greenville, GA one night, the thought occurred, "Are you going to continue driving this distance to see someone whom you're not going to marry?" Anita was certainly a beautiful young lady, but what made up Pete's mind to say she wasn't the one, was she lied when he asked her a very personal question.

Pete told Sonia about Anita, but the only thing Sonia knew was, Pete was hers exclusively, no strings attached. Once Anita returned from Job Corps, they would see each other very sparingly due to the adhesiveness Sonia applied to him, and eventually and shortly, they quit seeing each other. Sonia was extremely neat, clean and smart but too obsessive. Psychologically and affectionately, when he inwardly rationalized the future with Sonia, there wasn't a faint of doubt about the bond of future marriage. Demographically however, her family and social acceptance created a security fence that deferred marriage. He embraced the notion, seized and enjoyed the moment. Inner-racial dating during the mid 60s' wasn't very prevalent and wasn't warmly accepted and appreciated by the mainstream in Georgia. The city of Atlanta was more tolerable than say rural Georgia. In fact, when Pete was working at Sears, a supervisor related a certain area of Georgia, which was Cumming, Georgia, a Black-American truck driver wasn't allowed. During that period, Blacks didn't live there, and even in 2007, Blacks do not inhabit that racist area.

Pete was undaunted about anyone bothering them and recalls vividly during 1967, when he and Sonia were traveling south-west on Ponce De Leon on their way to Krispy Crèame Donuts when a convoy of White individuals laid on their car horns. But in his mind, he speculated it had been a K.K.K. meeting just breaking up that was held in Stone Mountain, GA, their headquarters.

Pete and Sonia's rendezvous was initially at his uncle's place, Peblo. This was his uncle's residence located in Tucker, Georgia. Interestingly enough, Pete's father's father, during the 1800s, purchased this property, and provided land for housings for all of his children. Fannie once described, her husband's father, Jack, as a very shrewd man but couldn't count too well. For each payment on the land, he would place a corn kernel into a jar, and, unfortunately paid twice for the property before officially owning it. This area is off Montreal Road, Tucker, Georgia. Pablo's place was on this property, as were all of Pete's father's sisters and brothers. To say Pete's grandfather was shrewd but couldn't count very well may seem a paradox. There's been an influx of opinions and perspectives to suggest a person who is well spoken and who commands the proper English of instruction is smart. The truest definition of intelligence and smart goes beyond the suggested and is principally gauged by the accomplishment of one's life, and not speech. However, a person should try to command the English language since it is widely perceived to gauge one's intelligence. Moreover, a person's self control under duress, is a precursor of underlining wisdom and intelligence. The true art of becoming wise is the execution of calm rationality under all circumstances.

After about a year of seeing each other in secluded isolation, they started going to movies, eateries and other places. Occasionally she drove his customized auto which naturally caused an abundance of stares, ooz and uhs. When she was a coiffure during her internship working on Ponde Leon near Sears, and Pete took her to lunch, people heads from the tall office building looked as though they were staring at something special at an amusement park. They would eat at a nearby fast food eatery. Immediately after ordering their food, a middle-age White man who, at the time, didn't look into the car as Pete got out to order their food; rather, had this fixation on the wheels of his car. They engaged in a brief conversation about the wheels, and after retrieving the order, Pete got into the car and said good-bye. Finally the man looked into the car with mouth wide opened and with owl-like eyes to behold white on white interior with the white and black décor of individuals. Sonia inquired, "Pete, did you see his face?" "Yes," he replied, causing laughter to overcome them.

Pete recalls Sonia's initial words when she entered his car, saying, "Your car is simply p-r-e-t-t-y!" Besides rendering "Thanks", he was quick to say, "I've never dated a girl that smoked." That would be the last time he'd see her smoke a cigarette until later years when he would stand her up. Ironically, he began to see other girls on the side, he used his then set aside logic, to 'sow his oaks.' However, he was sure she'd be the one to acquire his last name.

Sonia disclosed being from South Georgia, where prejudice was rampant and interracial couples had to sneak off to secluded areas to rendezvous. Living in a locality where such tolerance was at zero from surrounding officials and community figures, being in public would not be good for them.

How bold was Pete? Very! When Sonia's mother and step-father would go to South Georgia, Pete would spend the night there. Kid, after finding out what he did, lamented, "Have you lost your mind?" All Pete would do was chuckle. Her mother had to be suspicious when she had no dates come to their apartment. Sometimes her mother and her step-father, whom Pete dubbed "Big Dummy," would leave out of the community together during the early morning when Pete worked at Sears on Jefferson St., Atlanta, GA. Pete, looking peripherally, could see Sonia's mother staring at him, and would later find out the young man who owned and drove that classic auto was her daughter's boyfriend.

It all started when Pete refused to see her one Friday night when John and he had other plans. After standing her up, John and Pete went to a club called Soul City, and while there would meet three young ladies who would follow them to Patton Place Apts., hoping Ford would be there to entertain the third young lady. Unfortunately he wasn't there, so they bid farewell. After John and Pete departed, Pete drove by Sonia's to find she wasn't home. After not hearing from her since that Friday, on that revealing Sunday evening, Pete got his spirited first cousin, Rico, to call their home in hope to make it hard for her to ever get out. Admittedly, an angry and revengeful mind does not contain much validity, and some-times, produces a ton of inauspiciousness. Matter-of-factly, it was simply dumb and stupid, according to the admission of Pete. Rico would reveal their names, where they lived, place of employment, etc…To say the cat was out the bag would be infinitesimal, instead, Godzilla was out, aiming to maim and annihilate. Sonia's mother's suspicion was immediately confirmed, claiming to know who Pete was. While working then at General Motors in Doraville, GA, Sonia called to in-form Pete that Big Dummy and step-son, who Pete dubbed "Flicted," due to a deformed leg, had his gun looking for Pete.

Rico, who was as crazy and wild as they came, heard about this and immediately hid out in some tall weeds with bricks, readying himself to, using his words, "Rock-um."

Sonia's mother, Pete surmised, assumed he still worked during the day. But on that particular night, that Big Dummy could have done some damage to Pete, due to a short on his wire coming from the coil, with the car cutting off as he made it home safely. Rico, who stayed with Pete and Buck most of the time, was there when Pete arrived safely. "Man, I was ready to rock them," exclaimed Rico. "Did he ever come by?" Pete inquired. "No!" "We (Buck and he) didn't see anyone," replied Rico.

According to Sonia, her biological father's wife, her step-mother, mother and that Big Dummy called a summit, threatening to vote Sonia out of the family. Her step-mother reasoned, "How can you stand for him (Pete) to kiss you?" Sonia said nothing, only observing humbly and innocently. When it was all said and done, Sonia, sensing the sorrow her mother registered, she displayed a form of understanding but remained mute.

Pete kept this from his mother and father, knowing they would be flustered, frustrated, and angry.

Despite these threats, their love and temerity, kept them even stronger together, defying all odds. Pete's customized 1954 Ford continued to grow in popularity, becoming a conversation-piece throughout the Atlanta area, and even to-date, 2008, it comes up in conversations.

Kid, when he once lived next door to Pete, would ride to work with him to General Motors, he was a very cerebral, no-nonsense person, suggesting, "You know you have a 'show-caser', and cops are going to be stopping you, so therefore, keep your receipts on your mag-wheels and tires, etc."

A colleague of theirs at General Motors asked Kid to follow him after work to a girlfriend to help move some furniture around. Kelly, who describes his girlfriend as a sex symbol, apparently suffered from grandiose and substantial delusion.

After finishing this chore, Kid questioned, "Did you see that sex symbol?" "He's got to be kidding," Pete rendered laughingly.

Such laugher became solemn as they turned on the main street in Washington Park, when two White cops turned on their over-head lights for them to pull off the street and stop. "Let me see your license, please, then asked, where are you coming?" One of the cops asked.

"After getting off from work at General Motors, we helped a friend in Kirtwood re-arrange some furniture," Pete described.

The 390 engine had a three-two-barrel carburetor, street and strip racing cam with stock mufflers that caused the engine to reverberate similar to a pianist pressing keys as if he were disoriented.

"So that's where you're coming from." His partner, in a deliberate tone inquired, "Do you hear that?"

"Yeah, that's that cam he has in there."

The driver would ask, "Let me see the receipt on those wheels. After providing it, the cop perused it, handing it back and said, Y'all have a good night."

"Thanks, and you too, sir," Pete rendered.

Pete reflected his attention to the Bible when Jesus said to Peter, "Before the cock crow you will deny me thrice." Jesus' prophecy was point-on like the Kid's, as Pete marveled with much amazement, conveying him, "Man, you were right." Henceforth, there would be a myriad of occasions when Pete was stopped by cops for trivial to no apparent reason, but probably because he was a Black-American. One evening around 1968, driving near Kirtwood, an Atlanta cop stopped Pete, asking to see his driver's license and registration. After returning his credentials, commended, "You have a beautiful car." "Thanks!" was Pete's reply.

One of the most significant occasions came shortly after John had purchased and opened an Amoco Service Station on Second Ave. and Glenwood Ave. Atlanta, GA. Period: Oct. 1970. Buck and Pete agreed to come help organize the place. While driving the 1954 Ford on Second Ave. approaching Glenwood Ave., they entered the turning lane early. The service station was on the left side of the street. The left turning lane wasn't completely full, and Pete would enter it prematurely which was admittedly, illegal. After getting out the car, as customary, he and John would engage in horse-play. As Pete began boxing with John, momentarily, two White mean-looking cops accosted them, asking,

"Who was driving the 1954 Ford?"

"He went across the street to catch a bus," Pete responded facetiously.

"Y'all come out of there, we'll find out the owner and driver," one cop insisted.

"It's mine," Pete answered.

"All right, put your hands on the wall."

Although such lane-changing was illegal, but it didn't warrant the seriousness of being taken to jail. But considering Martin Luther King, Jr. being sent to the penitentiary on a mile misdemeanor citation, Pete wasn't that surprised. But was shockingly surprised later listening to one of the cops saying, "That's the nigger we see with that White girl...yeah nigger, we're gonna get you for something one of these days," declared one cop.

Admittedly, Atlanta has improved regarding race relations and police profiling, but during the 60's, it was next to intolerable. Ever since Rosa Parks refused to give up her seat to a White man, Dec. 1, 1955, slowly, things started to change. Thanks to the civil rights movement, and particularly Dr. Martin Luther King Jr., who was indeed a martyr.

To harbor unwholesomeness for a substantial period, only sickens one's morale, and brings cancerous results to a stalwart psychology. Additionally, whatever one regularly entertains psychologically, naturally becomes his or her destiny, whether good or bad. Therefore, to have a positive perspective and live optimistically and happily, one reaps a future forecast filled with an abundant harvest and prosperity. Sound observation teaches inauspicious circumstances of disturbed individuals, once they truly tap another's psyche, becomes tilt. One must develop an impervious mentality.

Th^{CHAPTER}ree

Facing Life's Challenges

IMMEDIATELY FOLLOWING HIS GRADUATION FROM high school, Pete was hired at Sears Warehouse on Jefferson St. in Atlanta, Georgia. After finishing high school in 1965, he was hired the same month, June, as a salesman/receiving clerk. Although he was elated being hired but would dance around certain issues proposed by one of his supervisors. If there was one quality that shone brightly about him, it was his character to befriend almost anyone. He wore often an infectious smile that was accompanied by a kindness and understanding that was nothing short of remarkable and outstanding.

His supervisor lived rather close to his residence and was deemed to have a hidden agenda and perhaps possessing pernicious intentions, based on conversations and unflattering remarks regarding Martin Luther King, Jr. Nevertheless, he seemed to like Pete a lot, and was never shy airing his views regarding civil rights. Early one morning during mid October, 1967, Sonia called Sears asking for Pete to reveal something extremely secretive.

Wardo, his supervisor, answered the phone and when he told Pete he had a telephone call, his countenance was noticeably affected. Sonia was obviously from South Georgia who possessed a southern drawl, but to Pete, likened to a child-like voice with a lot of likableness.

"You're wanted on the phone," Waldo related to Pete. No one usually calls him at work, and being that early, Pete surmised it was something very serious. "Hi Pete, this Sonia, I call to say….."In return, Pete assured her everything was going to be all right, and perhaps for the first unsolicited time, disclosed, "I love you," and that they would talk later.

Unsurprisingly, Wardo asked Pete, "Who was that?" "Just a friend," Pete replied.

During the mid 60's was the acme of the civil right demonstrations and civil unrests. A myriad of occasions Waldo would disclose to Pete, "See, he's (Dr. Martin L. King Jr.) a trouble-maker, huh, huh?" Pete, though, never agreed with him, but would nod and say, "Uh huh, I understand." Reticent on any true comment, Pete would inwardly say, *"Satan, why don't you shut your trap?"*

Besides Pete, James who was Black-American, worked in the Liquidation Center and eventually became a good friend of his. Though James was perceived as a good person by Pete, but he would party all night and would come to work in his party clothes, making him nothing short of a party animal. During the year, 1966, James introduced Pete to his girlfriend's sister whose name was Anita. James' girlfriend was Doris. Doris and Anita heralded from Greenville, GA., but were then living with a sister in an apartment in Carver Hills. James told Pete about a party Doris and Anita were having one Saturday night. Pete asked his lifelong best friend, John to go with him. Pete introduced John to James, Doris, Anita, etc…Both Doris and Anita whispered in Pete's ear how good-looking John was, and he immediately would say to Anita,

"If you want him, he's all yours." "I don't want him," she offered. However, Doris did want him and in spite of James, they became intimate. For years, James subliminally, blamed Pete for their break-up and the relationship that ensued between John and Doris.

While working a Sears, James and Pete, for a long period, were the only Blacks working in their department, and obviously, became very good friends prior to the party. The environment under which Pete worked wasn't real pleasant, but was nebulous, and at times, contentious. Hicks surrounded him, and sprang up like tares among a field of good seeds. Nonetheless, no one dared to physically challenge him due to fear and sound sense. The Liquidation Center was situated at the very front of the warehouse; whereas it was pretty immense. Pete would arm wrestle with all takers in the Liquidation Center, taking down the arms of everyone who challenged him. New male employees upon being hired were summoned to challenge him with no success. In a section of the Center where they tagged items prior to putting them on the floor for sales, A.Q., was easily taking down every challenger, until someone uttered, "Come on, Pete, we've found someone who can take your arm down. "No! That's okay," he responded as if he feared the challenge. "Are you afraid?" A voice rang out. Seconds later, Pete, who then stood about 5-10", and weighed around 175 lbs, placed his arm on the 4-wheel cart against the massive arm of A.Q., Pete observed arm-wrestling as 50 percent mental and 50 percent physical…And during the initial thrust, hold your own without being taken down, and simultaneously, ascertain the spontaneous strength of one's opponent, and then give it your all.

Pete felt the impetuous strength of A.Q., affirming inwardly, "He's mine." Pete purposely allowed A.Q. to put his arm almost down, and in the background, one could hear ooz's and ah's, and just as his arm went down, he seemingly, lifted A.Q.'s entire body off the floor whose arm hit the top of the cart very violently. "Did you see that?" Someone asked, A.Q. showed class and good sportsmanship, saying, "You got a good arm." Commendably, of all the staff there, he was a very likable person, exemplifying qualities most nowadays are lacking. And a matter of fact, he was definitely head and shoulders above the supervisory staff there.

Pete would sell his mag wheels to an employee there, and when they got to this man's house, who lived then in West End section of Atlanta, Pete could hear the apparent mother admonish him, "You better hurry and get back in here," after retrieving money from his house.

Admittedly, hicks were very prevalent there but had to respect Pete who carried himself appreciably and respectfully. Rayford, who was a workmate and bonfide hick, would banter Pete after showing him a picture of his girlfriend, offering, "Why don't you come go home with me to South Georgia, my grandfather would love to meet you.? I can't guarantee you'd come back alive but would come back in a box."

Apparently his KKK grandfather carried a predilection of ill-will toward Blacks, and who possibly had inflicted harm to Blacks over a period of time.

"Why don't you come home with me, I can't guarantee you'd get back whole," Pete touted laughingly.

Besides James, who was Black-American, Pete befriended Dade Neucomer, who was White and a fine young man who was neat in appearance and attitude. In stature, he was about 5-8", very stout with huge arms, and was an avid bench-presser. Dade could bench press 350lbs. He wasn't a match with Pete arm-wrestling but obviously could out-bench press him, something he never did.

During the late 60's, it was a widely held concept that most White males worked out with weights more than Black-

Americans. Whereas Pete would do sit-ups, push-ups and bar-pulls.

Dade invited him over to his house after work one evening. His garage had weights galore and a work-out bench. Pete helped spot him 350 lbs. with him pressing it 5 times. "Man, you're powerful," Pete raved. Pete could not equal his feat but did, from the floor, lifted 175 lbs, his weight. "For a person who doesn't mess around with weights, you're very strong," Dade commended Pete.

Dade, besides a fine person, was very personable and happened to be a clean and neat dresser. Of all the staffers there, he deemed James and Dade true friends.

While working at Sears Pete would learn Dr. Martin Luther King Jr. was shot and moments later it was confirmed he died from an assassin's bullet. How could Pete forget that particular rainy night, when shortly after hearing the news, he would drive to Perry Homes to see his aunt and cousin. The only information regarding his death was from a White man driving a Mustang. Though the crime was in Memphis, Blacks were frantically seeking any White male driving a Mustang in Atlanta, GA. Pete made it to his aunt's uneventfully but during his drive, his reflection was: Why would anyone want to kill M.L.K. JR.? To any decent, peace-loving people, he was a pillar of strength -- an institution and wealth of knowledge-- a paradigm and paragon image regarding Christendom. Most significantly, he was definitely the leader of not only Blacks, but of the justice-deprived and common individuals plagued by inequality.

While at work following Dr. King's assassination, Waldo's countenance was visibly lucid, he wore an expression of indifference and perhaps silent jubilation in his heart. How could Pete forget him calling this great man a 'trouble-maker?' Why didn't Pete argue in defense of Dr. King? His observation was quite simple, (To dicker with an idiot is the same as trying to bargain with the wind.)

The Bible points out and not to mention altruism, that is, to give up one's life for any one or a particular cause—there's no greater sacrifice. Though very young at the time, Pete was very shaken by the senseless tragedy by such a crazed individual and possibly conspirators.

Pete didn't attend Dr. King's funeral, but did view his remains in Ebenezer Baptist Church. Among the throng of people, he saw Harry Belafonte, Sidney Poitier and other luminaries. It was an unfortunate occasion with Pete being awestruck seeing so many dignitaries, but was personally gratifying being among such figures. Viewing the remains sadden Pete immeasurably, watching a tremendous figure who had done so much for the world who wouldn't live to see and realize his dream. He transcended the image of a great civil right leader but is greatly commended for his humanitarian deeds; moreover, the world didn't realize then, not even Pete, this great individual was a living symbol.

Theoretically, Pete thought, if there were ever a time an addendum could be attached to the Bible, the life and face of Dr. King should comprise many pages. In no way should any one equate a mortal to Jesus Christ but the parallel of their lives mirrored similarities. While Christ gave up his life for the salvation of the world, King gave up his life emulating the precepts ascribed to Christianity and his conviction, that, helping others, though he may be slain, would benefit Black-Americans, the poor and individuals deprived of equal opportunity. Simultaneously, knowing his place would be well cemented in the pantheon of God's elects.

In many of the eulogy letters Pete wrote, "We shouldn't be that concerned about the origin of life, we all came from God; we shouldn't be that concerned over the destiny of life, we shall all return to God; bracketed between life and death, we should be a loving service to humanity." Reflected in one of King's speeches, he encouraged individuals to not put importance on his academic credentials; rather, in the end, 'know that I tried to help somebody.'

Former Ambassador and Mayor of Atlanta, Andrew Young made mention recently how he and Dr. King would talk about envisioning their deaths by an individual or individuals, who, in Pete's observation, maybe orchestrated by then, higher authority. The mere thought of someone concocting ways to slay you would cause most individuals to desist one's course of living, or just relinquish their conviction or cause. Thankfully, our lives will be spared eternally according to the Bible...that is, losing one's life doing what is right, and particularly the will of God, one's life will be spared.

Luke, Chapter 9, Verse 24, Jesus declared, "For whosoever will lose his life for my sake, the same shall save it."

During the tumultuous 50s and 60s, Dr. King probably had Jesus' declaration etched in the lining of his heart and brightly laminated in his mind by not being fazed facing unenviable and formidable odds. Being sent to Reidsville Penitentiary on a minor traffic infraction; house bombed, by using his words, sin-sick White brothers; death threats to him and his family persisted...Presumably, the average, if not most Americans, would reject undertaking these daunting tasks that this great man and other civil right workers performed.

For any lay person, it is practically incomprehensible to actually conceive or plain imagine the cloud of threat that constantly loomed over Dr. King during his life, particularly during his involvement in civil rights. Again, this great man was exceedingly fearless, championing civil rights, and was unmistakably intertwined with God, just like others renown elects who preceded him. Hence, he was always mindful of many spiritual scriptures, especially II Corinthians, Chapter 4, Verse 16... "For our light affliction, which is but for a moment, worketh for us a far more exceeding and eternal weight of glory...While we look not at the things which are not seen: for the things which are seen are temporal; but the things which are not seen are eternal."

Yes, he knew and trusted God to deliver on His word; and most importantly, during his panoramic view at the mountaintop, God afforded him a preview of his spiritual destiny.

It's not unusual for God to reveal glimpses of the future to one who is intertwined with Him spiritually. The Bible illustrates innumerable occasions where God promised His elects noteworthy things that would be given them. Abraham's wife chuckled within when God said she was going to have a baby while she was in her 90s. Genesis Chapter 18:13 (And the Lord said unto Abraham, "Wherefore did Sarah laugh, saying, 'Shall I of a surety bear a child, which am old?'") The very next Chapter, 14, God reasoned, "Is any thing too hard for the Lord? At the time appointed I will return unto thee, according to the time of life, and Sarah shall have a son."

The same God who made good on His word to Sarah who did have a son, whose name was called Isaac, was with Dr. Martin Luther King, Jr. To say he had been to the mountaintop and had seen the coming and the glory of God, probably went fleeting by and over the heads of most people, being that many today are spiritually blind. To the spiritual-literates, they clearly construe this profoundness, "Though I may be slain by my sin-sick White brothers, yet I will live eternally within the presence and glory of the Lord." Clearly, the most important aspect of life is to die in the Lord and not out of Him.

Martin Luther King, Jr. (1929-1968), became a Baptist minister, and was also the main leader of the civil rights movement in the United States during the 1950s and 1960s. He had a tremendous speaking ability, setting him up to effectively express the demands of Black-Americans for social justice. His eloquence won the support of millions of people - Blacks and Whites - making him internationally famous. He won the 1964 Nobel Peace Prize for leading nonviolent civil rights demonstrations.

In spite of King's stress on nonviolence, he regularly became the target of violence. White racists threw rocks at him in Chicago and bombed his home in Montgomery, Alabama. Finally, violence ended King's life at the age of 39, when an assassin shot and killed him. Some historians observe King's death as the end of the civil rights era that began in the mid 50s. During his leadership, the civil rights movement won wide support among Whites, and laws that had barred integration in the Southern States were abolished. King became only the second American whose birthday is observed as a national holiday. The first was George Washington, the nation's first president.

King established his program of nonviolence on Christian teachings. He wrote five books: Strive Toward Freedom (1958), Strength to Love (1963), Why We Can't Wait (1964), Where Do We Go From Here: Chaos or Community? (1967), and The Trumpet of Conscience (1968).

Dr. King was born on Jan. 15, 1929, in Atlanta, Georgia. He was the second oldest child of Alberta Williams King and Martin Luther King Sr. He had an older sister,

Christine, and a younger brother, A.D. The young Martin was usually called M.L., his father was pastor of Ebenezer Baptist Church in Atlanta. One of Martin's grandfathers, A.D. Williams, also had been pastor there.

During high School, Dr. King did so well that he skipped both the 9th and 12th grades. At the age of 15, he entered Morehouse College in Atlanta. He became an admirer of Benjamin E. Mays, Morehouse's President and a well-known scholar of Black religion. Under May's influence, King decided to become a minister.

King was ordained just before he graduated from Morehouse in 1948. He entered Crozer Theological Seminary in Chester, Pennsylvania, to earn a divinity degree. He then went to graduate school at Boston University, where he got a Ph.D degree in theology in 1955. In Boston, he met Coretta Scott of Marion, Alabama, a music student. They were married in 1953. The Kings had four children, Yolanda, Dexter, Martin, and Bernice. In 1954, King became pastor of the Dexter Avenue Baptist Church in Montgomery, Alabama — the birthplace of the civil rights movements. King civil rights activities began with a protest of Montgomery's segregated bus system in 1955. That year, a Black passenger named Rosa Parks was arrested for disobeying a city law requiring that Blacks give up their seats on buses when Whites wanted to sit in their seats or in the same row. Black leaders in Montgomery urged Blacks to boycott the city buses as King was elected to serve as president. In his first speech as leader of the boycott, telling his Black colleagues: "First and foremost, we are American citizens...We are not here advocating violence...The only weapon we have...is the weapon of protest...The great glory of American democracy is the right to protest for right."

Terrorists bombed King's home, but King continued to insist on nonviolent protests. Thousands of Blacks boycotted the buses for over a year. In 1956, the United Supreme Court ordered Montgomery to provide equal, integrated seating on public buses. The boycott's success won King national fame and identified him as a symbol of Southern Blacks' new effort to fight racial injustice.

King, with other Black ministers, founded the Southern Christian Leadership Conference (SCLC) in 1957 to expand the nonviolent struggle against racism and discrimination. During that time, wide-spread segregation existed throughout the South in public facilities such as hotels and restaurants. Many states also used various methods to deprive Blacks of their voting rights. In 1960, King moved from Montgomery to Atlanta to devote more effort to SCLC's work. He became a co-pastor of Ebenezer Baptist Church with his father.

THE GROWTH MOVEMENT

IN 1960, BLACK college students across the South began sitting at lunch counters and entering other facilities that refused to serve Blacks. Civil rights protests expanded further, including major demonstrations in Albany, GA. Moreover, in the early 1960s, King became growingly unhappy that President John F. Kennedy was doing little to advance civil rights. Early in 1963, King and his SCLC associates launched massive demonstrations to protest racial discriminations in Birmingham, Alabama, one of the South's segregated cities. Police used dogs and fire hoses to drive back peaceful protesters, including children. Heavy news coverage of the violence produced a national outcry against segregation. Soon afterward, Kennedy proposed a wide-ranging civil rights bill to Congress.

Hence, King and other civil rights leaders organized a massive march in Washington, D.C. The event, called **The March on Washington,** was intended to highlight Black-American unemployment and to urge Congress to pass Kennedy's bill. On August 28, 1963, over 200,000 Americans, including many Whites, gathered at the Lincoln Memorial in the capital. The main highlight of the rally, King stirring "I Have a Dream" speech, eloquently defined the moral basis of the civil rights movement. The movement won a major victory in 1964, when Congress passed the civil right bill that Kennedy and his successor, President Lyndon B. Johnson, had recommended. The Civil Rights Act of 1964 prohibited racial discrimination in public places and education. King received the Nobel Peace Prize.

In 1965, King helped organize protests in Selma, Alabama. The demonstrators protested against the effort of White officials there to deny most Black citizens the chance to register and vote. Several hundred protesters attempted to march from Selma to Montgomery, the state capital, but police officers used tear gas and clubs to break up the group. The bloody attack, broadcast nationwide on television news shows, shocked the public. King immediately announced another attempt to march from Selma to Montgomery. Johnson went before Congress to request a bill that would eliminate all barriers to Southern Blacks' right to vote. Within a few months, Congress approved the voting Rights Act of 1965.

THE CHICAGO CAMPAIGN

BY 1965, DR. King had come to believe the civil rights leaders should pay attention to the economic problems of Blacks. In 1966, he helped begin a major civil rights campaign in Chicago, his first big effort outside the South. Leaders of the campaign tried to organize black inner-city residents who suffered from unemployment, bad housings and poor schools. The leaders also protested real estate practices that kept Blacks from living in many neighborhoods and suburbs. Essentially, King felt such practices played a major role in trapping poor Blacks in urban ghettos. Dr. King and local leaders organized marches through White neighborhoods. But angry White people in those segregated communities threw bottles and rocks at the demonstrators. Soon afterward, Chicago officials promised to encourage fair housing practices in the city if King would stop the protests. He accepted the offer, and the Chicago campaign ended.

As time advanced, violence continued against civil rights workers in the South, frustrating many Blacks, including members of the Student Nonviolent Committee (SNCC) leaders urged more aggressive response to the violence and began to use the slogan: "Black Power." That phrase irked Dr. King and many White supporters of racial equality. King however, repeated his commitment to nonviolence, but disputes among civil rights groups over "Black Power" suggested that King no longer spoke for the whole movement.

In 1967, King became more critical of American society than ever before. He believed poverty was as great an evil as racism. He said that true social justice would require a redistribution of wealth from the rich to the poor. Therefore, King began to plan a Poor People's Campaign that would unite poor people of all races in a struggle for economic opportunity. The campaign would demand a federal guarantee of annual income for poor people and other major anti-poverty laws.

Moreover in 1967, King impugned the action of the United States support of South Vietnam War (1957-1975). He observed the South Vietnamese government as corrupt and undemocratic. Of course, many supporter of the war denounced King's criticisms, but the growing anti-war movement welcomed his comments.

KING'S DEATH

WHILE ORGANIZING THE Poor People's Campaign, King went to Memphis to support a strike of Black garbage workers. On April 4, 1968, King was shot and killed. James Earl Ray, a White drifter and escaped convict, pleaded guilty to the crime in March 1969 and was sentenced to 99 years in prison. Ray later tried to withdraw his plea, but his conviction was upheld. Ray died in 1998.

People throughout the world mourned King's death. He was buried in South View Cemetery in Atlanta, Georgia. His body was later moved near Ebenezer Baptist Church. On King's tombstone the inscription reads: "Free at last, free at last, thank God Almighty, I'm free at last."

King's assassination generated immediate shock, grief, and anger. Blacks rioted in more than 100 cities. A few months later, Congress passed the Civil Rights Act of 1968, which prohibited racial discrimination in the sale and rental of most housing in the nation.

Years after King's death, some people still doubted that James Earl Ray acted alone. In 1978, a special committee of the U.S. House of Representatives reported the "likelihood" that Ray was aided by others. In 2000, the U.S. Justice Department announced that an 18-month investigation turned up no evidence of a conspiracy.

In 1974, King's mother was shot and killed while playing the organ at Ebenezer Baptist Church. The Gunman, Marcus Wayne Chenault, opposed black Christian ministers. He received the death penalty; but in 1995 was resentenced to life in prison without parole.

NATIONAL HISTORICAL SITE

IN 1983, CONGRESS passed a federal holiday honoring Dr. King. The day is celebrated on the third Monday in January. In 1991, the National Civil Rights Museum opened at the site of King's assassination in Memphis. The museum's exhibits cover the history of the civil rights movement. Dr. King's son, Martin Luther King, III., served as President of the Southern Christian Leadership Conference from 1997 to 2004.

Pete, 2007, can really appreciate Dr. King's past efforts regarding influencing the passing of the Civil Rights Act in 1964, prohibiting racial discrimination in public places and calling for equal opportunity in employment and education. The Chicago Campaign, Dr. King mobilizing civil rights workers in 1966, to call attention to the inner-city Blacks residents who suffered from unemployment, bad housing and poor schools. While demonstrators marched through White neighborhoods, they were greeted with rocks being thrown at them. Consequently, officials there promised to encourage fair housing practices in the city if Dr. King would stop the protests.

In the City of Angels, Los Angeles, California, 2005, a friend of Pete's who is White and a realtor, apprised him while she and a co-worker were scanning over old documents, she became aghast at the wording, purporting, "Do not grant loans to Blacks and Hispanics in certain communities." His friend, Suzanne, sighed, "I was simply appalled."

In 2007, it shows the country has come a long way from overt to silent discrimination and racism, but still hasn't come full circle to equality and impartiality. One can see the circle rounding, albeit, gradually. Yes, the recently elected mayor, Antonio Villaraigosa, in Los Angeles speaks volumes of change and the concept society is moving in the right direction.

Meanwhile, revisiting 1968, during Pete's tenure at Sears, he couldn't exactly comprehend the violence and tragedy that shook the country. Shockingly, some two months ensuing Dr. King's assassination, former Attorney General of the United States, Robert Francis Kennedy, was shot in Los Angeles on June 5, 1968, while campaigning for the Democratic nomination for president, and died the next day. In 1969, Sirhan Bishara Sirhan, a Jordanian-born Arab, was convicted of the assassination and sentenced to death. The sentence was commuted to life imprisonment in 1972 after the California Supreme Court declared the state's death penalty unconstitutional.

Robert F. Kennedy (1925-1968), served as Attorney General of the United States from 1961 to 1964 and as U.S. Senator from New York from 1965 to 1968. He was appointed Attorney General of the United States by his brother, John F. Kennedy, in 1963. He resigned from the Cabinet position in 1964 to run for Senate.

Robert F. Kennedy had entered the government in 1951 as an attorney in the Department, 1955, he was counsel for the Senate Permanent Subcommittee on Investigating attention in the late 1950s as chief counsel for the Senate committee that investigates management activities.

Robert F. Kennedy managed his brother's campaign for the U.S. Senate in 1952. He wrote "The Enemy Within," 1960, Just Friends and Brave Enemies," 1967, and "Thirteen Days,"

"A Memoir of the Cuban Missile Crisis," 1969. He was born in Brookline, Massachusetts, on November 20, 1925. He was a graduate at the University of Virginia Law School. His son, Joseph P. Kennedy, II of Massachusetts, served in the

U.S. House of Representatives from 1987 to 1999. Robert Kennedy's daughter, Townsend, served as Lieutenant Governor of Maryland from 1995 to 2003.

Beloved Robert F. Kennedy would have certainly won the Democratic nomination had he not been shot at the convention. Commendably, it is always praiseworthiness bestowed upon anyone who tries to make a positive difference that may affect the lives of others. Then the question for me is, why would someone want to kill such a person? The prevailing and pervasive question, even reflected in the lyric of some songs, beg: Why do the young have to die early? Realistically, why do they have to die at all by some crazed individual? "Why does God allow this to happen?" Pete offered, "God's specialty is dealing in the appearance of impossibilities." And regarding the allowance of things, "The pottery should never question the Potter." While it would be fool-hearted for anyone to think he or she knows exactly the way God thinks; He's too inscrutable and fathomless. James, Chapter 4, Verse 8 reads, "Draw nigh to God, and He will draw nigh to you." For sure, God does reveal some things to His elects.

Moreover, the word of God is clear when it quotes God as saying to Moses, "I will have mercy on whom I will have mercy, and I will have compassion on whom I will have compassion." Romans, Chapter 9, Verse 15, also, Verse 13 reads, "As it is written, Jacob have I loved, but Esau have I hated."

Romans 9:21 reads: "Hath not the potter power over the clay, of the same lump to make one vessel into honor, and another unto dishonor?"

Does this authorize one to stand nakedly and boldly at the throne of God and shake his or her fist at Him and question His sovereignty? An emphatic No, clamors.

Empiricism, biblical scrutiny and an intimate relationship with God, tap spiritual enthusiasm, causing one to discern

God will unquestionably reveal some mysteries beyond one's finite comprehension. Initially, one must love the Lord with all his heart and might; study the Bible, trust in Him and submit oneself to Him and live a moral life with a renewed heart and mentality; and depart from sin and evil. Psychologically, (There's a lot of noise in silence where a person's mind is cluttered with chaos and confusion.) Conversely, a person whose mind is stayed on the Lord, experiences much serenity and felicity. Jesus also says, "So as a man thinketh, so is he." Clearly, a person is a product of his general thinking or thoughts. Where one's heart is, his treasure is found. And to say God will reveal some things to His elects and individuals who trust in Him and live a godly life, is undeniable.

Fannie, Pete's mother was a classic example of this truth, the closer one gets to God the closer He'll get to you. While Pete's father and his friend Bussey, were driving from Chicago to Atlanta, GA, Fannie awoke during the middle of the night hysterically, saying, "Something bad just happened to your father." Awakening all six of her children, someone said, "He will be all right," and shortly everyone had gone back to bed. Confirmation of her vision or dream was later realized when their father didn't arrive until extremely late that Saturday, with his disclosing he and Bussey had an auto accident. Amazingly, at the same time God revealed the vision to Fannie, Bussey, while driving, fell asleep driving in Illinois, went off the road and landed in a cliff where their car rested. Just a few feet below was a precipice that would have spelled inevitable calamity. Pete's sisters and brothers didn't feel that anyone then lived as close to the Lord than Fannie and consequently, they would revere her admonitions when she advised against certain things. More often than not, during her reluctance and admonitions, things didn't go well—while testimonials are plentiful from her children.

The Kid, Pete's older brother, kept encouraging him to try to get hired at General Motors in Doraville, GA. A company at which he started working since 1964. Admittedly, Pete had grown tired of working at Sears, having to deal with many hicks and abject characters, and despite the career benefits, it was time to exit. During September 1968, G.M. was taking an influx of applications, and heeding his brother's advice, on the same day filling out an application he was hired.

He was awe-struck at the size of the complex and the varying facilities strung in series assembling automobiles. Admittedly, he became very nervous during his first job assignment, placing front-end parts and brake hoses on Chevrolets, Oldsmobiles, and Buicks. Eventually, on the assembly-line, he was assigned to the hub job, placing the left side hubs and some brake lines on some of the frames. A simple job, but a job many didn't like, but Pete kind of liked it, despite the repetition. There was a hydraulic-lift to lift the hubs from crates. Just prior to the end of the night-shift, both left and right side hub workers, would lift hubs manually, mounting them farther up the line in advance for the next shift. Meanwhile, Kid worked about 20 yards away to his left and was the very first worker to touch the chassis as he would read the manifesto, place it on the chassis; write the number on it and place a stabilizer bar on some of the chassis. At the time, there were two shifts: the day and night shifts. Pete used to razz him, saying, "The day shift guy can write better than you." He would fire back, "Bull shit." And both would chuckle. In actuality, they both wrote numbers well, but Pete thought Kid wrote better. Ironically, both wrote the numbers leaning on a left-ward slant.

Fannie questioned the move from Sears to General Motors: "Why would you (Pete) quit a job like Sears with great future benefits and go to General Motors?" The interjecting Kid reasoned, "With the money he makes at General Motors, he can create his own future benefits too." The astute Fannie didn't verbalize it but quietly agreed to the transition and trusted same. Education, notwithstanding, but Fannie was not only a person favored by God, but she comprised immeasurable discernment and common sense.

Meanwhile, Pete wasn't too happy about working the night shift, realizing it would affect a lot of his time with Sonia. In fact, occasionally he would pretend to be sick and be permitted to be excused so he could go home to be with her.

As he ruminates over the span of time, the 60s marked the signature of the ages, involving dynamics and revolutionary turns.

In sports, 1964, Cassius Clay became heavy weight champion of the boxing world by defeating Sonny Liston, a feat many thought was next to impossible which indeed, shocked the world. Shortly later he changed his name to Muhammad Ali. Pete observed this phenomenal athlete, the greatest heavy weight boxer ever to grace the world, due mostly to his intellect, athleticism, nimbleness and grace. As a sport favorite, and someone with stern conviction, Ali was definitely his favorite athlete of all times. Though brass, cocky and controversial at the time, and despite the toughness and savagery of boxing, Muhammad hated no one and didn't possess an iota of malice in his heart towards anyone. What separated him from the average athlete? Pete believed the greatest source of power or strength to overcome was exceeded by the force of will and reliance in the Almighty God. And yes, the hicks at Sears despised Ali and would murmur in disgust when Ali would defeat a White opponent.

CHAPTER
Four

Recalling Portions of the Sixties

DMITTEDLY, FROM 1967 TO 1970, Pete was far removed from much of the current events, that is, things that perhaps piqued the interest of common folks. He did, however, come out his capsule to lend interest to man landing on the moon — something that caught his attention and interest considerably. There were brief thoughts, on his part, to enlist into the Air Force and learn mechanics and to fly, since he was one of about thirteen of his high school classmates to take and to pass the Air Force test during his eleventh year of school.

In LIFE magazine, January 17, 1969, the caption read, "Our Journey to the Moon," written by astronauts Frank Borman, Jim Lovell and Bill Anders, was very amazing. They titled their story, 'A science fiction world — awesome, forlorn beauty.'

Excerpts from astronaut Frank Borman: "The most incredible sight of the flight — of my entire life — was my view of the moon. We had just completed the turn that put us into lunar orbit when we passed the terminator on the moon.

Darkness and light — and saw below us the hostile face of the moon. I felt as if we had been transported into a world of science fiction, with incredible lighting and awesome, forlorn beauty. The moon was so desolate, so uninviting, so completely devoid of life, or anything to indicate that there ever had been life. Nothing but this great pock marked lump of grey pumice. For us, lunar orbit was the busiest time of the flight. I was flying our attitude-control thrusters because we had to keep our windows aligned to perform all our tasks. Jim Lovell was making navigational checks and verifications on the surface of the moon, and Bill Anders was the busiest of all. He had a flight plan and a photo plan and he had scientific observations to make. He was so conscientious about all of this that when I wanted to take a picture of the earth as it came over the horizon he objected. "Gee, Frank," he said, "that's not on our photo plan." Eventually, I was able to talk him into giving me the camera so I could take pictures of the earth over the lunar landscape.

The three accounts of these extraordinary astronauts were mind boggling, fascinating and enlightening. Their patriotism aside, it took courage beyond imagination to just entertain the idea, and to actually undertake such enterprise, is stupendous in the first degree involving valor and audacity.

What was Pete doing at the time during the initial announcement man had successfully landed and walked on the moon? He had rendezvoused with Sonia, and on his way home after stopping at a convenient store for snacks, engrossing the store, gazed heavenward, looking for the moon, and began to marvel, sighing meditatively and inwardly, "What a feat."

Despite man's phenomenal accomplishments, naysayers will forever earn their titles, and Pete's grandfather on Fannie's side, his mother, was no different. Thing is, though a superb individual, was impractical on many fronts, James Jacob herald from White Plains, Georgia, who was espoused to Pete's grandmother, Mrs Willie B. Jacob...A union that bore six beautiful girls who blossomed into beautiful women. Fannie would narrate her father as a working man, but was on the lazy side, telling of the time when Pa, whom they dubbed, had a mule to help out with farming. This mule wasn't fed properly and was emaciated and effeminate. As Pa would sit in a chair with leather harness straps in hands, and would say "Git-up mule." snapping the straps. The more he would snap the straps, the more the mule did nothing. In fact, the mule would just lie down at times. When Pa would say get-up and snapping the straps.

Pa was a tall handsome man, about 6 feet 2 inches, and weighed about 220 lbs. with a very fair complexion, thick mustache and black coarse hair. During World War 1 it was very rare for Black-Americans to travel overseas in the Army, but those who did were relegated to performing menial chores. Many felt Pa was mistaken for White during his travels overseas due to his extremely light skin.

In fact, Pa didn't have documentation of himself being born. While at any official place, when asked his date of birth, he exclaimed, "How do I know, it was in the dark." Pete would take him to Mc Donald's for morsel and would read to him on a hamburger wrappings, 100 percent beef. "It ain't no more pure beef, they cross-breed cows with the colts, lions, tigers, etc..." Laughter was unavoidable. To Pete, Pa was indeed the theatre of humor. But realistically, he wasn't largely a senseless, but a superstitious person, who to-date, should be credited to a patent which the tobacco company earns profits even today. He once asked Kid to write to the tobacco co., suggesting to mix Prince Albert tobacco with regular cigarette tobacco. He didn't get a response, but shortly after, the tobacco co. produced a blend of tobacco called Half & Half.

He was highly superstitious, and ironically, didn't believe in having mirrors in his house and didn't want anyone to take his photo. Many a time while walking from Washington Park to Scottsdale, GA to go to the Post Office, and say a black cat crossed his path, he would mark three times with his foot and would turn around and return from which he came.

In 1969, Pete asked him, "Pa, what do you think about man traveling all the way to the moon, and walking on it?" "Blame fool, they ain't went to no moon, they're probably somewhere over in Arizona." Obviously, Pete's laughter was almost incessant.

Years later, Pa passed away, and when Pete related his passing to Sonia, she expressed sympathy, saying, "I've never met your grandfather, but do recall you all laughing at things he would say and do."

CHAPTER Five

Man in the Mirror

AT THE AGE OF FIVE on one hot summer day in Decatur, Georgia, Pete and his four-year-old sister, Sally, sought relief from the heat. "Let's go in there and buy some ice-cream?" "All right," she replied.

Shortly ensuing purchasing and receiving their ice-cream from that Decatur ice-cream parlor, they attempted to sit down to enjoy their treat. "Git up from there you can't sit down there and eat, you have to go outside," shouted this elderly white-haired White lady. Pete was frightened that he had done something terribly wrong. Adjacent to the ice-cream parlor was a grocery store where Fannie has gone to buy groceries. She had pointedly instructed them to stay in the car.

When she returned to the car Pete was a bit reluctant to tell her what had happened in the ice-cream parlor, knowing that she had told them to stay in the car. Nevertheless, his urge to ascertain what he had done wrong in that parlor outweighed their action by leaving the car.

Consequently, she wasn't sore at them for leaving the car but admonished that they obey her henceforth...Then

47

she went on to attempt to explain that Blacks couldn't sit and eat at certain places reserved for Whites. When Pete's reiterated 'whys' rang out, she stammered to say, "Some White people don't feel comfortable around Black people."

This incident occurred in the early 50s. At such a tender age, Pete wondered why his money was good enough to purchase the ice-cream but wasn't good enough to sit at the table and eat it? He truly loved his mother and knew she was sincere in her explanation, but he wasn't quite satisfied with her response. He perceived immediately the idea the world wasn't right, something was wrong, and a change was necessary.

A few years ensuing this incident, Fannie told about a period during her courtship with their father, about racism being more rampant. During the 1930s, Hayman worked for the Pullman Co. in Atlanta, GA on Dekalb Avenue. He worked there for thirty-three years. A railroad occupation was one of the most elite and prestigious jobs men coveted. Being the natty and prideful person they'd always known their father to be, he wore tailored clothes and kept up his annual, renewal ownership of a Buick and masonry membership.

On a lovely, quiet and serene evening while driving around enjoying the ambience, as well as each other, he casually drove into a service station for gas. A young White man, who was the service station attendant, accosted him and asked derogatorily, "Who car is this, boy?" "Mr. Whitford's," he rendered wittingly. Of course Mr. Whitford was himself, whom he assumed was his boss, A.K.A, supervisor. Such derogatory quip in today's society, or depending on the idiosyncrasy of an individual, would have stirred emotions of anger, likely leading to an altercation, especially by being put down while with his wife or lady friend by, a disrespectful, null and void knuckle-head, who perhaps was bred and fed racial hatred. And when it does occur, it demoralizes and degrades one's manhood. But given the time and era in which this occurred, the response Mr. Whitford's was opportune and appropriate. Moreover, such response in any era was suitable. Such remarks defended his manhood and simultaneously, averted a hostile encounter. After all, it took nurtured, commendable innate traits of strength and discipline on the part of an individual to avoid what seemingly, is a no-way-out confrontation. To be successful, one must be perceptible initially to provocations and things that lead to confrontations. And being a practitioner of tolerance and self-control, the application of good judgment, followed by concern, communication and concession must be exercised. The Bible is practical on this subject as it reads in James Chapter 1, Verse 19. "Wherefore, my beloved brethren, let every man be swift to hear, slow to speak, and slow to wrath."

Mr. Johnson lived a few houses down the street from Pete. Mr. Johnson was the uncle of Margrette, the Kid's wife. Self-employed in Landscaping, he always had a positive word to say to people, regardless of how he felt during any given time. Someone remarked in the community, "Mr. Johnson could grow grass on a rock." He once offered, "Brother Buck, Pete's brother, some White people remind me of cement poured in a bucket, in order to get it out you have to tear up the bucket." Incidentally, God called him home February, 1994. Sally, Pete's sister, along with the power and auspices of God, had the main street in Washington Park re-named in his honor.

Pete and Buck would cringe and cower during a story a neighbor related. Mr. Osburn, who lived three houses down from Pete's was born in 1903, near Loganville, Georgia. They were petrified with interest to hear him describe this Black-American man, Frank, who used to live with his mother and father. Mr. Osburn was an only child between his mother and father.

Frank was formerly married to a very fair complexioned Black-American lady. In fact, she appeared almost white,...

according to Mr. Osburn, Frank had an obsession for White women. He even served time for breaking and entering a house trying to get to this young White lady. One day Frank was at this shop and overheard some White men discussing going into town the following evening, one of whom had a daughter. That night Frank was trying to enter the window of the house. Half way through the window this woman had a gun and shot Frank, a glancing wound. After jumping from the window, he fled home. Frank made out that he was asleep in bed. There were seemingly about a hundred White men standing outside their house. When they inquired of Frank, his father, who had always been undaunted, responded. "All of you can't go into my house."

He, however, allowed two of the men to enter. Moments later, they brought Frank out. Approximate one-hundred yards away was a Mulberry tree, where he was hanged.

During Pete's formative years residing in Georgia, he experienced an assortment of different characters and idiosyncrasies but refused to bend from the teaching of his parents and the Bible. How do we change the world in which we live? By being a bright beacon, exhibiting patience care and concern toward fellow brethren and cloning Christian character under all circumstances. In order to prosper and enhance impressive qualifications within, one has to rise above the level of racial prejudice, hatred and racism.

One former co-worker in Georgia once whispered in his ear, "You know, Pete, my father doesn't like Black people, but said he likes you." Pete had assorted feelings; he wanted to feel proud, but couldn't and was bothered by the remark. Perceiving the father perhaps a racist, or a person whose racial perspective was tainted with ignorance, and lack of understanding. One other occasion Pete befriended a Georgia State Trooper, whose name was Sam. He occasionally joked with Pete about race, and would say, "Pete, you're such a nice guy, whenever you get to heaven, God's gonna paint you white." You know, seriously, my mom and dad did teach that Blacks were inferior to Whites." Pete liked this friend primarily due to his honesty and recalls vividly when he perished in an auto accident on his way to work. It was misty weather that night, his car overturned and landed on its top. He died almost instantly, sustaining a broken neck. Recalling their dialogues during the past, Pete didn't go to the funeral, but did view his body, and couldn't hold back tears. Afterward, the Sergeant came to Pete and related, "Pete, Sam's mother and father told me to tell you thanks for your visit."

More often than not, a kind heart is the proper medicine for an unkind spirit, and in cases bringing conversion to the incorrigible. What is racism but a charge to God that some races are unequal to others and that He errored during creation? Additionally, what is prejudice but a benign cancer that eats gradually away at humanity, specifically to those possessing it, until it eventually consumes the whole?

It has been said the only one's who can hurt you are those closest to you because they know most about you. And to say Pete liked his trooper friend is quite simple, he put on no airs and showed exactly where he was coming from. And with his saying God would paint him white when he got to Heaven was obviously racist, abject and injurious. This young man had been fed garbage and rubbish. His parents embraced a lynch-men-like mentality, were badly tainted with misunderstanding and misguidance.

But to take an accurate and truthful look in the mirror, reveals true nakedness. Everything one utters doesn't all come from the heart, but the continual display of one's actions... mirrors the heart. Unfortunately, the parents of the real-live narratives involving such individuals weren't fed the fruits of wisdom, understanding, knowledge or virtue. Looking into the law and mirror of the Holy Bible, Philippians Chapter 4, Verse 8, doesn't mention or advocate prejudice and racism, instead, encouraging... "Whatsoever things are true, whatsoever things are honest, whatsoever things are just, whatsoever things are pure, whatsoever things are lovely, whatsoever things are of good report; if there be any praise, think on these things."

Pete's father had to take a hard look in the mirror and re-evaluate his life and make a decision pertaining to his way of life when their mother gave him an ultimatum—either he joins the church and quit his worldliness or she was leaving him. This happened around 1945, just after the birth of Dot, her third child. His love for her prompted him to desist his way of life and to hold on to the woman he planned to live out the balance of his natural life with.

The Pullman Company moved from the Atlanta area to St Louis in 1953. Hayman loved his job immensely and wanted to transfer along with the company and did so after a long dialogue with Fannie.

At the time, Pete was only six years old. His father's occupation was a truck builder, requiring him to work on the wheel of trains. Later, he retired, and when the trains from Avondale would go by late at night and whistle. "You hear that train?" Hayman would say.

Fannie was just 29 years of age when Hayman transferred to St. Louis. That meant she had to function as a single parent. During that era, she was a housekeeper for three White ladies, all of whom were sisters, to help out financially. Obviously, their father would send money home weekly and, visited about once every two to three months.

Right after his transfer he wanted Fannie to visit him around Thanksgiving of 1953. Fannie would get her mother to stay with her children. She lived a block away. She would take Buck, the baby with her. Each child loved their grand-mother, but despised her authoritarian ways. The children happily welcomed their mother back with warm delight during her one-week stay with their father.

Their mother was not only a good Christian but good-natured. On one occasion back in the late 1930s, one very hot summer day a robust Black man, with mud on shoes, boarded the bus and dared, "I ain't giving my seat up today for nobody." Immediately following his outburst, there was a noticeable silence. Many Black passengers displayed smirked faces, whereas Whites wore astonished and shocked expressions. This made their mother overwhelmingly filled with humor and laughter.

Meanwhile, Washington Park was continuing to grow in what it was known for, its meadow and cemetery, and Scottdale was reputed for its violence...So much so, someone once dubbed Scottdale, Dodge City and Washington Park, Boot Hill.

Pete's interest in his first year of high school grew increasingly indifferent, and became influenced by his sister's boyfriend brother, to play hooky and cut classes. At Hamilton High, Jack and Pete would skip classes all day, until it was time to go home. Pete influenced John to do likewise. Jack didn't like John joining them, remarking John was weak and frightful. After answering the roll call in their homeroom class, they'd return when it was time to go home. That was until they were caught in the boiler room.

John and Pete got hellacious whippings from their parents. It was good they were caught. Despite missing a tremendous amount of time skipping classes, John and Pete never did stay back a year in any particular grade. There were some schoolmates who didn't get promoted and had to repeat a grade.

John got fed up with the notorious reputation of Scottsdale and transferred to Trinity High School, Decatur, Georgia. Being his best friend, it didn't take much to influence Pete to join him.

Attending school in Scottsdale, Georgia was synonymous to entering an active war zone whereas survival was a blessed taste. Keeping concentrated attention on school academics was secondary to mere avoidance of assaults by individuals. Robert Shaw Elementary School and Hamilton High School were all-Black schools. Adjacent counties, schoolmates had to be bussed there with much displeasure. Of course, most of the assailants were males residing in Scottsdale, GA. Many times, a new male schoolmate would come from a different residence who didn't reside in Scottsdale, more often than not, would be attacked.

On one particular day, after boarding the bus, the bus-driver stood outside as a group entered the bus and demanded the coat of a male student. The trembling guy didn't only give up his coat, but urinated on himself from fright. A female student remarked, "Look! He peed on himself."

One particular day, a resident of Washington Park was sitting in the Cafeteria at a table preparing to eat, nearby when a group from Scottsdale, walked up to him and slapped this individual very violently, knocking him and his food to the floor. There were many similar incidents. Attacks weren't just confined to prey emanating from neighboring counties individuals, they became domestic and deadly. On one weekend an individual residing there, used a shotgun, to shoot to death another individual, splattering his brain and blood on a street alongside of Hamilton High School. That Monday, someone from Scottsdale showed others the blood and brain residue.

Pete was transferred to Trinity High School during his tenth year of high school, which he liked immensely. Sally Mae transferred to Trinity as well. Historically, she and Pete have always done what one another did.

There's one exception she stopped bird-hunting. One day they played sick or just didn't go to school. Retrospection and empiricism are clear that God forbids the killing of innocent birds or any wild-life just for the sake of killing. Being thirteen months older than his sister, Pete was around 10 years old during this particular time. Like Nimrod, he was a good hunter whose marksman-ship with a sling-shot was nothing short of incredible. After having claimed 6 robins, they ventured deeper into the woods in search of additional prey, but what they experienced was indeed a revelation that would leave an indelible imprint on their minds . To-date, it remains inexplicable what they saw, or how it got there. They happened upon, what appeared, a shepherd. "Look! Where did he come from?" Sally asked. This old man stood about 6 feet 2″ tall with olive skin and a beard that came to his sternum; featuring a staff that was about 2 feet taller than he and wore biblical attire, a robe with a rope around his waist. This shepherd appeared to be from the era of 32 A.D.

Understandably, they ran out those woods with break-neck speed until they'd reached their house. It took a good while, after stopping before catching their breath, to discuss what they saw. Despite adolescence, they were old enough to distinguish between right and wrong, but the significance of this revelation didn't dawn on them until later in life with Sally questioning, "Why did God allow me to see this shepherd?" Pete rationalized, "Because He knew one day you would be kind-hearted and caring toward the elder in the community—lending assistance to the needy."

Maturation and insight likened the revelation to that of Saul while on the path to Damascus, perhaps on horse back, when this bright light shone on him. The horse on which he rode, became frightened by its brilliance, reared up on its hind legs which caused Saul to fall to the ground. Saul became temporarily blinded for three days. While on the ground the voice of the Lord exclaimed, "Saul! Saul! Why persecutest thou me?" The shuddering Saul inquired, "Who art thou Lord?" Affirming Jesus, "I am Jesus whom thou persecutest: it is hard for thee to kick against the pricks."

The story of Saul's harassment and persecution of Christ's disciples is well documented in Acts, Chapter 9. Saul's name would later be changed to Paul, who wrote sixteen books of the New Testaments.

Underlying Pete's revelation, some individuals suggested it was Francis of Assisi, a Saint, 1182-1226. He was something like an animal rights advocate who would talk to them. Assuredly, regardless of who it was, God and only God allowed them to see this Biblical figure probably to shake Pete's senselessness of killing birds. And with retrospect to this shepherd or angel Sally and Pete saw, the message was crystal clear: Quit annihilating birds. How could one prey on innocent birds or perform senseless, destructive acts? Checking the index of life, ll Corinthians, Chapter 5:17 clarifies, "Therefore if any man be in Christ, he is a new creature: old things are passed away; behold, all things are become new." Simply, old mental make-up dies; born, is a renewal Christ-like make-up.

Admittedly, at this juncture in Pete's life, he was too young, wild and adventurous to pause and take a look in the mirror and, illogically, such revelation didn't deter him from hunting. But as he gradually got older, the desire to hunt faded completely. Also, his interest in school faded as well. He wanted to just pass, complete high school and land a good job with good retirement benefits. Emulating his older brother, Kid, he was employed at a pharmacy, delivering prescription medicine. Such employment afforded him the means to purchase his first automobile, a 1953 Plymouth.

Six
CHAPTER

It's Never Too Late For Justice

HE PRESS TELEGRAM NEWSPAPER, A local Southern California newspaper, printed January 11, 2003, "It's a dream come true." Reporting Illinois Governor frees four from death row. With just three days left in office, Gov. George Ryan's cited they were tortured by Chicago police into falsely confessing in the 1980s, declaring their cases "a perfect example of what is so terribly broken about our system."

Ryan cited the pardons as part of a three-year campaign to reform Illinois capital punishment system, which began when he declared a moratorium on executions in January 2000.

He also cogitated commuting the sentences of 140 other death row inmates to life in prison.

Gov. Ryan pardoned Madison Hobley, Stanley Howard, Aaron Patterson, and Leroy Orange, stating police tortured them into confessing to murders they had not committed. Each was on death row at least 12 years. One had been on death row for 17 years.

Minorities live daily, even in 2007, with apprehension of injustice and inhumane propensity leveled by those who aren't of color. Profiling by law enforcement or by law enforcement officials lead to an assortment of evil and mistreatment. The penal system isn't too friendly to minorities, Latinos, and those of color. Capital punishment is a prime example showing the disproportionate number of Blacks on death row. For one, the death penalty is cruel and unusual punishment and should be abolished once and for all. There was once printed on a bumper sticker the words "Does putting to death a killer for killing make killing right?" Additionally, the assertion it is a deterrent to crimes is only an assertion that does not hold an iota of truth. Some states have put a temporary halt to the imposition of the barbaric penalty accountable to innocent individuals who had been put to death. DNA today, is freeing individuals wrongly incarcerated for crimes they didn't commit. Once an individual has been put to death for a crime he or she didn't commit, man or the law is powerless to recall a life.

The death penalty is simply wrong due primarily to the power that be in determining who should or shouldn't receive it. It's pure discriminatory. A Black man is more apt to receiving the penalty for committing a crime against a White person compared to a White individual receiving the penalty when committing a crime against a Black person.

In 1972 Furman vs. Georgia decision, where the United States Supreme Court outlawed the penalty, citing it was cruel and unusual punishment the way it was applied, one Justice used the wording arbitrarily and capriciously used, made it wrong.

Since then, Capital Punishment was reinstated during the mid 70s after proponents drafted new laws to make it equally applied. Although it was ratified and approved by the United States Supreme Court, it (death penalty) is still arbitrarily and capriciously applied, making it today still cruel and unusual punishment. Poor people, underprivileged, docile, under-educated, and non-personable individuals don't stand a jot of a chance when caught in the web of the system while facing the ultimate penalty. It's abolition and outcry is heard over the entire world—a civilized world—purporting NO to such savagery. Just taking a glance in the mirror, proponents morally should acquiesce to its abolition.

CLASSIC MURDER

WHENEVER CAPITAL PUNISHMENT is carried out by states, it demeans society's morality and character and puts itself on the same level of the perpetrator who commits murder. The common question begs, "Does putting to death a killer for killing make killing right?" Of course, it doesn't! Can the innocent or victims claim their redemption? No! Their lives cannot be restored. However, those who are responsible should face the appropriate penalty of life imprisonment without the possibility of parole, which, in itself, is a slow agonizing process psychologically.

What is there to say towards the rehabilitated imprisoned? The very reason and concept for states to imprison is: retribution, rehabilitation and deterrence. Just the concept of being caged up is the crudest form of punishment imaginable. Some individuals choose death rather than be confined permanently. There are the incorrigibles who are unfortunately better served to just expire during confinement rather than be set free in society, jeopardizing the innocent.

Obviously, anyone confined for any reason for any crime he didn't commit should be extricated immediately. Conversely, anyone confined and convicted of a capital offense where the presumption of guilt isn't very strong, and there is obviously strong signs of rehabilitation, special merits and consideration should be given thereto. Thanks to DNA, many who are wrongly convicted and confined and didn't commit crimes are being set free.

Criminalistic ways of living is absolutely wrong and should never be practiced or even considered by anyone. Realistically, there is no profit in the development of gangs and criminal living, such a way of life leads inevitably to a shorten life punctuated by either imprisonment or the graveyard. The establishment of one's future fore-shadows his contemporary lifestyle. Therefore, in life one's mental focus should stay on growth in higher learning educationally, absorbing morality, godliness and successfulness, causing to develop a future forecast impregnated with much promise and profit.

When considering the history of people of color, it is conceivable most oppose capital punishment since they were on the very end of it. However, this generation shouldn't be accused of what happened yesterday to people of color. In fact, commendation is appreciably acknowledged to those individuals in power who have the courage and prosecutorial empowerment to bring to justice those culpable of past wrongdoings against Blacks. Bringing to justice, Edgar Ray Killen, an ex-K.K.K. for his part in the slayings of three civil right workers some 41 years later, indicates brightly the signature of time. The USA Today Newspaper reported on Wednesday, June 22, 2005, the caption, "Ex-K.K.K. member guilty in killings," (Jury agrees on lesser charge, not murder.)

The article purported a former Ku Klux Klansman was convicted of manslaughter on Tuesday, June 21, 2005 in the notorious 1964 murders of three civil rights workers—41 years to the day after they disappeared.

The jury make-up of nine Whites and three Blacks, after two days of deliberation rejected murder charges against Edgar Ray Killen.

Kellen, 80, was stoic during the verdict reading, he was immediately taken into custody. Kellen, used a wheelchair, because his legs were broken in a logging accident in March, 2005. It has become widely accepted that God doesn't cause calamities, but allows them. Just maybe there was an underlining unspoken message in this particular case, including especially his conviction of manslaughter, netting a 60-year sentence for his part in the abject murder of three innocent men, Mr. Chaney, Mr. Schwerner, and Mr. Goodman.

The case is a positive gesture by a Southern state to atone for justice denied during the civil rights era. In 1994, Mississippi convicted Byron De La Beckwith in the 1963 murder of state N.A.A.C.P leader Medgar Evers. In Alabama, Frank Cherry was convicted in 2002 of killing four Black girls in the 1963 bombing of a Birmingham church.

Moreover, another despicable case, the 1955 slaying of 14-year-old Emmet Till in Mississippi Delta, has been reopened. June 2005 his remains were exhumed in order to have an autopsy.

The paper read: A biracial local coalition pressed last year for justice in the Philadelphia case. Tuesday, they were elated to gain a measure of closure for a crime that was the basis for the 1988 film, Mississippi Burning.

The verdict "signifies this county has dealt with its past and is ready to move on to the future," said Leroy Clemens, President of the local N.A.A.C.P. and Co-chairman of the Philadelphia Coalition.

The slayings of James Chaney, Andrew Goodman and Michael Schwerner were one of the most talked-about crimes of a bloody era. They had been registering Black voters when they disappeared. Their bodies were found in an earthen dam 44 days later. They had been beaten and shot.

Killen and 17 others were tried on federal civil rights charges in 1967. Seven were convicted — none served more than six years — and Kellen was freed after a mistrial.

Prosecutors asked Judge Marcus Gordon to let the jury consider a lesser charge of manslaughter. Murder requires proof of intent to kill. Manslaughter requires only proof that a victim died during a crime.

Schwerner's widow, Rita Schwerner-Bender, praised the decision, but said the jury's failure to find Kellen guilty of murder "indicates that there are still people among you...who choose not to see the truth."

Former Mississippi's Secretary of State and Philadelphia native Dick Molpus, became the first state official to apologize to families of the slain men in 1989, hailed the verdict as a kind of exorcism.

"Should this have been done 40 years ago? Absolutely. Is there more work to be done? Clearly. But this is one significant step toward redemption for Neshoba County and for the state of Mississippi," he said.

Such prosecution of injustice done in the past is an encouraging and positive sign in restoration toward racial harmony and equality. Memory may never purge the senseless violence inflicted to those of color and Jews in the past, but cases like Mr. Kellen brought before the judicial system, serves as gigantic notice that abject violence committed by any one currently or historically will not be tolerated. Racial utopia isn't as far away as many individuals may think, but considering the not-too-distant past, there's obvious improvement which seems to grow with time. And to say memory may never purge past victimization in the past, there's a Higher Order to whom all should consult for forgiveness and simultaneously, forgive others for past transgressions. Biblically, when God forgives one, He doesn't only forgive, but expunges transgressions and remembers them no more. Man, who is made in His image, should emulate His ways and goodness.

About one month following Mr. Kellen's conviction, published July 26, 2005, in the Daily Breeze newspaper with the caption "Justice is sought in '46 mass lynching." Civil Rights: Re-enactment draws attention to the Georgia case in the wake of last month's conviction of Edgar Ray Kellen.

The stage mock, though surreal, where the gunshots were firecrackers and the blood was from plastic bucket of barbecue sauce and costumes were ordinary clothes with some participants wearing white masks and a white sheet, their appearance didn't evoke an actual portrayal of the real culprits in 1946.

The acting may have appeared naïve, but their underlying purpose of the re-enactment of the lynching there on the bank of the Appalachia River in which two Black women, one seven months pregnant, and two Black men, one a World War II veteran, were killed by a mob of White men 59 years ago, July 25, 1946 - July 26, 2005. No one was ever prosecuted, and organizers of the event say they wanted justice.

The outcry for justice comes soon after the conviction of Edgar Ray Killen, a one time Ku Klux Klansman found guilty in the 1964 killings of three civil rights workers in Mississippi just a month earlier.

In Moore's Georgia, State Rep. Tyrone Brooks, one of the re-enactment, called on the U.S. attorney to get involved. "We cannot find closure until there is prosecution," he said. "We cannot find conciliation until there in prosecution."

Clearly, there is always difficulty in trying such old cases, ranging from deceased witnesses; memory of prospective witnesses; willingness of witnesses to testify, to obtaining old transcripts.

The Moore's Ford lynching occurred 18 years before the Mississippi Killings, but Brooks said he believes as many as five of the perpetrators were still alive.

The rally of the re-creation of the anniversary comprised mostly of Blacks. There was a crowd of about 150 from the First American Baptist Church in Monroe, GA., where Rep John Lewis, the Rev. Joseph E. Lowery and other prominent Georgia civil rights veterans spoke, along with the Rev. Jesse Jackson of the Rainbow/Push Coalition.

The participants led a caravan of reporters and other attendees on a tour of important locations in the killings, including the farmhouse where one of the victims had an altercation with a White farmer, the jail where he was held and the spot where the shootings occurred. KKK in the crowd congregated, some stood on the railings of the bridge that now span the Ford to get a better view.

Now speaking through a megaphone, Brooks related how the four victims were dragged from the car and down to the riverbank, where they were shot. The woman might have been spared, he said, but one made a mistake of addressing one of the attackers by name.

Then the re-enactors, all Black, began; some wearing white masks to indicate that they were white Klan members.

"Remember, these are not real actors, these are home-grown folks who want to get the word out about what happened here in 1946," Brooks said.

During that period, the Moore's Ford lynching made national headlines, and fortified President Harry Truman's support for civil rights legislation. Truman ordered the FBI to investigate, but they, too, were met with hostile silence. They were unable to crack the case, although Brooks said, he thought the FBI's 1946 report contained enough evidence to prosecute.

Turning back the clock to the barbaric inhumane treatment of Blacks and Jews by sin-sick mentalities of low-life individuals today, is hard to comprehend such acts taking place. Jews and Blacks suffered persecution, humiliation, intimidation, assault, and murder in the past for no apparent reasons. Although we're living in a forgiving society, a more tolerable and intelligent society, whenever impropriety occurs racially, the clamor of protestation is usually loud and strong. Society is growing weary where its youths are victimized by cops who are, in some cases rogue or just unskilled to perform their profession professionally. Memory is fresh in Los Angeles where a 13-year-old Devin Brown, who was joy-driving, and who was perhaps driving erratically, drawing the attention of police and was later shot dead. Afterwards, it was learned the car in which little Devin was driving was stolen, but wasn't known stolen preceding the shooting, according to reliable sources. Expectedly, the senseless, reprehensible shooting drew outrage by citizens who wanted to know why this child had to die? Please spell out a clear justification. Despite frayed nerves and elevated pulse rates, the public remained calm under the circumstances. While imploring for answers, one mom asked, "Why kill our babies?"

Seven

Common Practice Glance

IN PETE'S PAST, HE WAS a late learner of maturity, but instead lived on the somewhat 'wild side', but realistically wasn't a bad person. Sound observation teaches, a person who isn't in control of his temple, certainly isn't in control of his life; rather, he or she is bedeviled by the power that be. Meaning, that person is controlled by circumstances and not disciplinary soundness or doctrine and thus, becomes subjected to an assortment of evils and wrongdoings. Unavoidably, whatever one commonly practices is what one commonly becomes. For instance, if a person commonly tells lies, he becomes a person of mendacity.

Observing the positive side: Larry Bird, who played for the Boston Celtics, has gone on record to say he wasn't very skillful concerning basketball; he admitted he couldn't jump very high and didn't have much speed. What made this extraordinary man legendary was what he commonly practiced. He was said to shoot hundreds of shots behind the free-throw line and the three-point line. Consequently, he established himself to become one of the most feared shooters the NBA has ever witnessed. Legendary Hall of Famer, Magic Johnson, also went on record to say Larry Bird was one of the best basketball shooters he has ever faced and went on to say each time Larry Bird would shoot the basketball, he knew it was going through the hoops. Larry Bird's success is directly linked to common practice.

Vince Scully, the Hall of Fame announcer of the Los Angeles Dodgers, didn't reach national prominence without common practice. He is arguably the best at his craft, his tapestry of calling games is an art of beauty, elegance and implacableness, thanks to common practice.

Buck, Pete's brother who worked at an Atlanta engineering firm, is credited to assisting in the construction of the Bonaventure Hotel in Los Angeles and many of the completed buildings in Atlanta, GA., didn't become a master designer of suit-wear without intense study and common practice. Though not nationally or internationally known, but those who know and have seen his designs can attest to his designs as pure elegance and stimulated beauty. He once conveyed to Pete, "God gives everyone more than one talent...And gives everyone a talent with which will feed him or her, but one's truest talent, that person will nourish. Sometimes, a person can live almost a lifetime before learning his or her truest talent, and conversely, sometimes, one's truest talent is known as a child, in many cases."

In Buck's case, his truest talent was known as a child. Whenever Pete and John scheduled a shopping spree during their teens regarding the purchase of clothes wear, John would say to Pete, "Don't forget to bring Buck." Of course, he'd pick or had to approve their selections.

Make no mistake about it, Buck does not subscribe to the styles of GQ Magazine, but does say, a minute portions can hold veracity. For instance, GQ touted; Tiger Woods was wearing pleated pants that's two sizes too big. Then GQ went on to criticize some NBA basketball players, naming some, this writing won't list, questioning, "Why do such players wear suit jackets the size of a wedding tent?"

Buck designs all Pete's suits and advises him on casual wear. But what he did say about GQ assailing Tiger Woods' attire, especially slacks being too big with pleats, "I wouldn't listen to that slop, Tiger looks good in those pleated slacks, in fact, he has the perfect physique to fashion any clothes-wear. I wouldn't listen to that shuck," he emphasized. He went on to say, "There is no particular wrong or right way the NBA ballplayers and others wear their suits because fashion is very subjective. What is elegant to one beholder is non-elegant to another. They wore oversized suits in the 30s, which you called the un-constructive appearance, but personally, I liked my suit tailored to fit. You can tailor clothes to drape off an elephant. I think GQ was trying to sway guys to revert back to the early 60s where men wore jackets too tight and pants that looked like scuba-diving suits."

He would say to Pete, "Do you recall our father railing the pants we wore in the 60s? He called them 'punk pants.' Then Buck went on to provide an intriguing analogy: "If a person wanted to get to Heaven that person would study the Bible…conversely, if a person wanted to be point-on in his or her attire, that person would study the styles of the 30s and 40s, because those stylists studied fashions as if it would get them into Heaven."

Buck cherry-picks their fabric from stores around the world, but a lot of it is purchased at B.Black and Sons in Los Angeles, California, a store that had been in business since 1946. The proprietor there showed Pete a graphic on President Lyndon B. Johnson, dated August 20, 1971, when Austin Exclusive Tailors tailored a suit for the then-President. Buck likes B.Black and Sons because the store carries fabrics with weight, giving the suit a scorch-like appearance.

Meanwhile, eyes that have focused on Buck, surmised arguably, that he was not only a great designer, but perhaps the best-dressed man contemporarily and maybe ever lived, thanks to common practice.

Denzel Washington and Harrison Ford didn't become the best at their craft without common practice and study. Needlessly to mention, there are an infinite list of individuals in the pantheon of notables who can attest to their success accountable to common practice.

It is very important to take notice of what one commonly practices in life; otherwise, one could wind up in a sticky web of regret. A person who practices racism will likely become a racist. A practitioner of hatred, one usually becomes a hater. Usually, the ingredients to reformation to such inauspicious development in life are: God, time, maturity, prudence and sound doctrine. Once one becomes reformed, he or she experiences contrite and ruefulness having whiled away or languished in time to inauspiciousness and stupidity. What plagues most nowadays, is to grow up too slow or get old too soon. Analogically, slow, denotes lack of knowledge during one's formative life where one thinks he knows everything and deep down feels that he knows, but in essence, knows nothing. Referring to old or age denotes knowledge, wisdom and experience where one takes a panoramic retrospective at earlier life and starts regretting with utterances of ifs, shoulda and coulda, and starts measuring the balance of his life. Therefore, advice to young individuals growing up, first, place total trust in God and stay focused on higher learning and academic. Moreover, chose wisely one's company, evaluate their action, aspirations and endeavors. Always choose the company similar to your own traits and goals. (Clearly, use common-sense.)

RACE THEME CONTINUES

THERE CAN BE much written and said on what strains racial harmony…The biggest wedge that splits racial divide is pure hatred and disregard towards those who are different. Many individuals residing in the United States of America contain mixed blood which makes racial hatred more appalling and incomprehensible. Some people believe in their living the true meaning of which this great country represents. United means tied to one, one God, indivisible with liberty and justice for all. Unmistakably, the Bible is clear where it reads "To say you love God and hate your fellow brethren, and God, whom you've never seen, makes one a liar." The first commandment is to love God with all of your heart and soul…The second commandment is to love your neighbor as yourselves. (One's fellow brethren.) Realistically, we are all equally different with varying talents endowed by the wonderment of God. Once a person starts disliking creation, (oneself) he automatically despises the Creator, placing that peculiar person on precarious grounds.

The very essence of America was constructed by our ancestors, whose blood, sweat, tears and deaths should always be appreciated and remembered. Despite past atrocities and inhumane inflictions, America has come a long way to right itself of the reprehensibility of past wrongdoings.

The Daily Breeze newspaper, Sunday Oct. 20, 2002, a local Los Angeles paper, carried an article with the caption: "Two Are Convicted in 1969 Slaying During a Race Riot." "Trial: Former Mayor Is Acquitted of Aiding White Gang that Shot a Black Woman to Death in Pennsylvania." Although, the former Mayor was acquitted, there were two other men who were convicted in the shotgun slaying of a young Black woman when race riots ripped apart York, PA, in 1969. The paper read the verdicts all, but closed the books on a crime that had haunted the city for more than three decades. The former Mayor, 68, cried after an all-White jury verdict was read, and later said the tears were for prayers. The two men convicted were sentenced to 10 to 20 years in prison.

The riots were launched by White and Black youths, leaving the young Black woman and a White patrolman dead.

The former Mayor, Charlie Robertson, and two other men were tried in the death of Lillie Belle Allen, a preacher's daughter from Aiken, S.C., who was gunned down by a White mob on July 21, 1969. Robert Messer-Smith and Greg Neff were convicted of second-degree murder and face sentences of 10 to 20 years in prison.

The ion-unsolved case is almost completed...Of the 10 White men charged in Allen's slaying, six pleaded guilty earlier and await sentencing.

Shockingly, prosecutor said Robertson, who then was a policeman and went on to become re-elected Mayor twice, handed out ammunition to at least one of the gunmen in an effort to get even for the shooting of the patrolman three days before Allen was slain.

According to the paper, Rick Knouse testified that Robertson gave him 30.06 rifle ammunition and told him to "kill as many" Blacks as he could.

Robertson admitted shouting "White power!" at a gun rally the day before Allen's killing, but denied other accusations.

It is mentally incomprehensible why anyone would aid and abet in the killing of any innocent human being. This society needs law officers to serve and protect, not arrogantly wield their power to randomly kill individuals, depriving them of life. There needs to be very rigorous psychological test given to prospective police officers before being hired. My understanding of the need for testing came from a reliable source, who teaches computer training to police officers that, some are known skin-heads and society-rejects who have no business policing themselves, let alone humanity. No way is it true that officers aren't honorable, reputable and trustworthy...Empiricism has it, a small minority are observed rouge, repugnant and reprehensible.

Pete has always claimed having 2 lifelong best friends. Besides John, Charles was his best friend; a friendship, like John's has stood the test of time.

Charles lived then in Washington Park, which was about 4 miles east of down-town Decatur, GA. Having known each from childhood, the two have never fought or exchanged harsh words, including John.

There was one notable weakness about Charles and that was, under pressure, he would oblige an interrogator.

While at school during high school study, about 5 schoolmates slipped to the store at Hamilton High. Pete and Charles were among the five that particular morning during school hours. They were busted on their way back from the store by the principal, who directed each to his office to question each why they broke school rules: panning the 5 schoolmates, Mr. Harvey stopped at Charles and offered: "You seem like a nice boy, who encouraged you to go to the store?" "Pete!" he replied. Pete developed mixed feelings, wanting to laugh in disbelief, Charles would implicate him and shocked over his candor. Nevertheless, the principal didn't spare any of the five by inflicting several lashes to their behinds, but seemed to whip Pete the hardest.

Another noteworthy occasion that tested their friendship, and simultaneously, exposed impropriety if not profiling on behalf of Lilburn, GA police.

The summer of 1967, while driving on Highway US 29, on their way to a party with exhilarated expectation but was thwarted with frustration, humor and disgust. Besides Pete and Charles, Fred and Boy accompanied them. At the time, Pete had had his driver's license revolted due to receiving excessive tickets, and of course, had no business driving. His Customized 54 Ford had stock mufflers which meant they weren't loud like a hot rod.

They had just entered Lilburn when someone exclaimed, "There's a police car," which was parked just off the main street. As Pete drove he shouted "Don't look back at them!" That warning came a bit late as Fred turned his head, looking at them. "Here they come," someone informed. Having followed them about one mile, Pete turned on his right signal and drove up to a convenience store and got out and entered the store. Meanwhile the Lilburn Police car drove just past the convenience store and parked.

Immediately Pete beckoned for Charles to come into the store. He reluctantly agreed. "Man, you know I cannot get back behind the wheel of that car?" Pete reasoned. "Dog, man, dog, he uttered.

After returning to the car with Charles underneath the steering wheel, Pete suggested, "Let's try the-it-won't-start trick. But, don't let the engine start when trying to crank it," Pete admonished. During several attempts to start the car, Charles and Pete got out the car and raised the hood. Charles re-entered the car and repeated trying to start the car as the two policemen watched similarly like two eagles studying their prey. Given a reasonable amount of time, Pete impatiently sighed, "Let's go."

Proceeding to travel east on US 29, only this time Charles behind the steering wheel. Those Lilburn cops also re-entered US 29, stalking them much like a cat on a bird, only this time, the cat, after their travel about a mile and a half, would turn on its lights for them to pull over and stop. The area where they stopped was dark and foreboding, which sent jittery and uneasiness to their psyche.

The two White cops approached the car with flashlights, as one stood on the right side who shined his flash-light into the car, and one shined his light in the face of Pete and Charles and demanded, "Let me see your drivers license, boy."

Charles nervously obeyed with the cops re-entering their patrol car then immediately walked back to the 1954 Ford and ordered Charles, "Follow us!" Their nerves became frayed and shaken, not knowing what would unfold next as the officer kept Charles' drivers license.

They would follow them to a medium-size brick building resembling a police sub-station. The officer ordered everyone out of the car and into the building, as one demanded to Charles, "All right, take everything out of your pockets." Pete was perceptive enough to know where Charles was headed and inquired, "Why are you locking him up, what did he do?" "You got loud mufflers on that car and unless you have $35.00, we're going to lock him up," the cop insisted.

Pitifully, altogether the four of them didn't have the disclosed amount, while Charles asked, "Can he come, too?" Referring to Pete. "Naw, only you." Pete had surge of humor but suppressed not even a hint of a smile but couldn't help but to notice the obvious apprehension, madness and sadness etched in Charles' face.

"Well, can we make a call, please?" Pete asked. The officer allowed Pete one call. At that time John and Pete were dating two sisters who originally came from Greenville, GA. They lived with their sister and brother-in-law in Carver Heights in Atlanta, GA. Pete's hunch was on target as he dialed the number with Doris answering and immediately put John on the phone. Pete explained what happened with John saying,

"That's stupid driving that car in Lilburn, GA, whether loud mufflers or not, with the number 2 on your tag, they're gonna stop a car like that. He agreed to come get Charles out of jail. John would visit his grandmother who lived just past Lilburn, Georgia. He later advised, that those cops there had a reputation for stopping people driving through there with license-plates other than 16.

The three of them waited seemingly forever for John to arrive to bail Charles out as they sat outside the police station. At that time, John had a 1955 Ford. Being a practitioner of sound logic and maturity, John would wait for Pete's brother to get home from General Motors and showed up in Kid's Volkswagen.

Pete contemplated challenging the conduct of the Lilburn police practice, but decided to let by-gones be by-gones, even though sensing conspicuous impropriety and bias existed.

CHAPTER
Eight

Presidential Figures

HE DAY THAT CHANGED AMERICA and brought tears, shock and sadness to our nation, was Nov. 22, 1963. At school during social studies, the principal's voice came over the intercom, "May I have your attention, please! A short time ago we learned that President John F. Kennedy was shot along with Governor John Connally...We will keep you informed as soon as news developes." During a short period ensuing the first announcement, a second message from Mr. Mark which related that President John F. Kennedy had died, leaving most classmates numb, glum and dejected.

Pete reflected upon the time when his mother told him that some people don't like being in the company of Blacks, then thought to himself, "The world isn't right and needs a change." President Kennedy was one of the most beloved presidents of our time. Why would anyone want to assassinate or murder such a fine person, or any person? The thought resonated mentally, 'The world needing a change', in fact, this cruel event exacerbated an already diabolical world.

Sadness and solemnest befell our country, seemingly the world stopped and there was substantial doubtfulness as to the direction it would take once it resumed. This was one of the most powerful men in the world and who happened to be one of our most popular presidents. He traversed color-lines and was beloved by practically everyone. No president or first lady has graced and gleaned the respect, love and admiration as the Kennedy's. They were standards by whom other predecessors or successors are measured and certainly emulated. It is an axiom that a classy person does not harbor pettiness, division and racial hatred; rather, that person is constantly preoccupied, promoting decency, respectfulness and wholesomeness.

The sad drama was culminated by the live, on-screen shooting of Jack Ruby, killing the alleged lone assassin, Lee Harvey Oswald. It was like a fiction movie with each plot occurring unexpectedly and drama, surrealistically, unfolding, right before the eyes of the world. Pete's young mind couldn't comprehend the gravity of what was happening. But one thing he all-too-well knew: violence wore an abject face of irrationality, irresponsibility and insensitivity.

President John Fitzgerald Kennedy was assassinated in Dallas, Texas on Nov. 22, 1963, by 24-year-old Lee Harvey Oswald. A few hours later, Lyndon Baines Johnson was sworn in as President of the United States by Federal Judge Sarah T. Hughes.

Those who weren't in attendance during the funeral procession watched on T.V. sadly and attentively as the horse and carriage transported President Kennedy's coffin to Arlington National Cemetery. Anyone who is old enough to remember with any measure of love and compassion, has a mental, photogenic catalogue of the scene of Jacqueline Kennedy, with her two children, Caroline and John Fitzgerald, Jr., in front of Senator Edward Kennedy, Attorney General Robert Kennedy and other members of the immediate family. As the President's remains were carried from the church, John, who was three years old, saluted his father's coffin as it passed.

As time passed, the country grew to cope with and digest this distasteful event. Antecedent and during this epoch, there had been and was civil unrest plaguing the country; racial harmony was akin to a kaleidoscope, ever-changing. The pattern that precipitated these unrests was always similar and involved injustice.

The wheel of the Civil Right Movement was set into motion by Rosa Parks, who, on Dec. 1, 1955, refused to give up her bus seat to a White passenger. This incident caused the United State Supreme Court to repeal bus segregation. The mid-century was the elimination of discrimination against U.S. Negroes. In 1954, the United States Supreme Court unanimously ruled segregation of public schools unconstitutional. Many Black activists as well as Whites launched an attack on discrimination in all its forms. The main objective was equal opportunity for all in employment, voting, housing, education, and public accommodations. They staged boycotts, rent strikes, sit-ins and freedom marches to achieve their goal.

On August 28, 1963, some 200,000 staged a march on Washington as the country heard from speaker after speaker. But most notably, we heard Dr. Martin Luther King Junior's (I Have a Dream) speech which still resonates in our minds and memory. It was recognized as one of the best speeches ever. Such accolade came from President John F. Kennedy, when someone from the White House asked his response? "I've heard that before," referring to another speaker. But when specifically asked about Dr. King's speech, his sharp response came in the form of three words, "He's damn good."

Ensuing the speech, Dr. King and other dignitaries met with the President to discuss their objectives and concerns. About three months later, President Kennedy would be assassinated. Lyndon Baines Johnson assumed office of the president. In 1964, Johnson was elected President, with Hubert Humphrey as his vice president. President Johnson, by many individuals, was observed as a good president. His credentials ranged from declaring war on poverty with his Great Society program. Congress passed his comprehensive Civil and Voting Right legislation. The Economic Opportunity Act of 1964...Created Head Start, the Job Corps, and Vista (Volunteers in Service to America.) Federal aid was given to elementary and high schools, more scholarships were offered to the poor, and a Teacher Corps was formed. Immigration and consumer protection legislation was passed. In 1965, Medicare was established to give health insurance to the aged.

Despite these noteworthy credentials, the blight on President Johnson's record was his decision to commit U.S. troops to active combat in South Vietnam, which put a pall over his administration. History deemed the war in Vietnam as unpopular and perhaps, unjustified and unscrupulous.

Taking a snap-shot on a few former presidents with reference to opinionating perspective: Besides John F. Kennedy, President Jimmy Carter was a good president. Besides heralding from Pete's native home state, Georgia, he was a very moral man who displayed charisma and personableness. He was a welcomed change from his predecessors, Gerald Ford, and particularly Richard M. Nixon, who resigned from office in disgrace and disrespect. Americans voted democratically to embrace a change due to the republican's distrustfulness, particularly the Watergate scandal. What smeared the image of the executive branch during Nixon's second term in office was the scandal that emerged in June, 1972, with the arrest and ensuing conviction of several men, two of whom were former White House aides and an official of The Committee to Re-elect the President. They had broken into the Democratic National Headquarters in Washington D.C. As FBI, Justice Department, and Senate Committee Investigators looked into the break-in, it became clear that other key members of the White House staff, and possibly the President himself, may have participated in or approved of this and other illegal campaign activities and tried to hid information from investigators. Investigations were slowed by the President's refusal to turn over all evidence requested by the Justice Department's special prosecutor. The Senate Committee, and a constitutional crisis on the question of the limits of executive powers and privileges seemed imminent. In May, 1974, the House Judiciary Committee formally opened its inquiry into possible grounds for impeachment of President Nixon.

Compounding damages to the executive branch was the resignation of Vice-President Spiro Agnew in October, 1973. Agnew stepped down from office rather than face indictment on charges of tax evasion, acceptance of bribes, and involvement in other illegal activities. Representative Gerald Ford of Michigan became the new vice-president.

When Richard Nixon resigned from office in 1974, Gerald Rudolph Ford became the United State's thirty-eight President. Ford graduated from the University of Michigan in 1935, and became a football and boxing coach, and continued his studies at Yale Law School, from which he graduated in the top third of his class in 1941. He then practiced law in Grand Rapids, Michigan. He served in the Navy for four years during World War II and later was elected to the House of Representatives from Michigan's Fifth District in 1948.

His presidency spanned about four years; but ended with a close race against James Earl (Jimmy) Carter. President Jimmy Carter was born in 1924 in Plains, Georgia. He attended Georgia Southwestern College and the Georgia Institute of Technology in 1941 and 1942 and entered the U.S. Naval Academy in Annapolis, graduating in 1946. He remained in the Navy until 1951. During his tenure in the Navy, he worked with Admiral Hyman Rickover whose influence on him was, according to President Carter, maybe second only to that of his parents. Carter left the Navy in 1953 as a lieutenant. After his father's death in 1953, he entered the family business and became a successful peanut farmer. He married Rosalyn Smith of Plains, Georgia in 1947 and they had three sons and one daughter. In Plains, Carter became active in community affairs and local politics. In 1962, he won a seat in the state senate. He was noted as having a liberal voting record during his two senate terms. In 1966, he ran for governor of Georgia against segregationist Lester Maddox. Carter lost but ran again in 1970, this time winning both the primary and the general election.

To validate that Jimmy Carter, our thirty-ninth President was not only a good president, but a good individual, recently the Nobel Committee recognized his incessant efforts to find peaceful solutions to international conflicts. Moreover, a champion at promoting economic and social development; promoting civil rights; the 1978 Camp David Accord. Currently, he's directly involved with Habitat For Humanity.

Most notably, he opposed going to war with Iraq, suggesting to explore a peaceful mean to solve an effusive and dangerous matter.

How did Pete feel about the war in Iraq? He opposed it with reservation and stipulation. Unless there was undisputable and conclusive evidence Saddam Hussein was stock-piling weapons of mass destruction, no way should the war be waged. Only under the circumstances of gathering support of the community relating to the U.S. allies and predominantly non-friendly countries, should war be waged. Sure the United States was changed forever on September 11, 2001, when everyone watched in aghast as the two airplanes operated by terrorists plowing into the Twin Towers in New York. The U.S. citizens and residents who continued to try to grasp with comprehension and imagination what took place as the ill-fated aircraft that went down in Pennsylvania. There can never be enough *valors ascribed to* those American men and possibly women who possibly altered the course of the aircraft.

A commendation was in order to President Bush for attacking Afghanistan with intention to annihilate the terrorist, particularly Bin Laden. Unmistakably the search for such villain continues and should until justice has been dealt to him.

Pete thought one rationale for attacking by the U.S. was to show to any rogue or so-called bully country, that we are a county that will not cower when attacked; that it is a super power whose will is to exact swift and severe judgment and punishment on any would-be aggressors.

According to a report in USA Today, gathered by a CNN Gallup Poll, when asked was it a mistake for the United States to send troops to Iraq? For most Americans, sending U.S. troops to Iraq was a mistake, additionally the majority felt it made the nation less safe from terrorism. Ironically, it was like the war in Vietnam, when a majority of Americans didn't support the justification for that particular war. Although major conflict and fighting are officially over, with a new Iraqi Government in place, insurgents are still killing U.S. and coalition forces. Kidnappings and beheadings are becoming common occurrences, which put a bitter taste and dislike in the minds of all warm-blooded Americans.

USA Today cites 54 percent of Americans think it's a mistake for US troops occupying Iraq. This gallop poll was taken March 23, 2003-June 23, 2004.

Returning to Presidents, Pete dared to rate current and past Presidents of the United States, but does provide an analytical assessment of point of reference.

Much credit is given to Abraham Lincoln for the Emancipation Proclamation, which was declared in 1863 and took effect in 1865. Having the audacity to free the slaves was intestinal fortitude, and obviously unpopular with some mentally tainted Whites at that time. The hand-prints of his assassination by John W. Booth were all over his propensity towards African and Black-Americans. The adage, "Why does the good die young?" has many facets of point of reference, while there is no specific answer other than to generalize that their time was designated by God. Abraham Lincoln once said, one could take 150 Blacks men and defeat an entire continent of people. Besides recognizing the prowess of Blacks, he also recognized Blacks were loving, caring human beings; individuals of intelligence and sensitivity.

During this writing, Pete sadly reports the death of the U.S. fortieth President, President Ronald Reagan, who died June 2004. Oftentimes when a President serves two terms in office; he's very popular and is usually doing a good job. President Reagan was well-liked by Pete, although he wanted former President Jimmy Carter to be re-elected. President Carter, though a very good and caring person, was deemed a bit weak. He probably loss re-election because of the hostage crisis in Iran, when Iranians stormed and seized the U.S. Embassy in Iran.

It was perceived President Reagan was a western cowboy who sported a quick draw and a volatile temperament. This was derived from his previous stints as an actor and followed him to the White House. Pete liked Mr. Reagan for a number of reasons. He stood tall like a pillow of strength; liked his candor because it was akin to a whistle — straight and unquestionable.

On February 6, 1911, Ronald Wilson Reagan was born to Nelle and John Reagan in Tam Pico, Illinois. While in high school in nearby Dixon, he worked his way through Eureka College. His major was Economics and Sociology, and he played on the football team. He acted in school plays. Ensuing his graduation, he became a radio sports announcer. During a screen test in 1937, he won a contract in Hollywood. Two decades later, he had appeared in 53 films.

His first marriage was to Jane Wyman, from that union, they produced two children, Maureen and Michael. Maureen passed away in 2001. In 1952 he married Nancy Davis, who was an actress, and they had two children, Patricia Ann and Ronald Prescott.

In 1966 he was elected Governor of California by a margin of a million votes, and was re-elected in 1970. Reagan won the Republican Presidential nomination in 1980 and chose as a running mate former Texas Congressman and United Nations Ambassador George Bush. Voters, vexed by inflation and by the year-long confinement of Americans in Iran, swept the Republican ticket into office. Reagan won 489 electoral voted to 49 for President Jimmy Carter.

On January 20, 1981, Reagan took office. Just 69 days later he was shot by a would-be assassin, but quickly recovered and returned to duty. His grace and wit during the dangerous incident made his popularity to soar.

Imaging himself gracefully with Congress, Reagan obtained legislation to stimulate economic growth, curb inflation, increase employment, and strengthen national defense.

He embarked upon a cause of cutting taxes and government expenditures, refusing to veer from it when the strengthening of defense forces led by a large deficit.

A renewal of national self-confidence by 1984 helped Reagan and Bush win a second term with an unprecedented number of electoral votes. Their victory turned away Democratic challengers Walter F. Mondale and Geraldine Ferraro.

In 1986, Reagan obtained an overhaul of the tax code, which eliminated many deductions and exempted millions of people with low incomes. At the end of his administration, the Nation was enjoying its longest recorded period of peacetime prosperity without recession or depression.

On the foreign policy front, Reagan sought to improve relations with the Soviet leader, Mikhail Gorbachev. He negotiated a treaty that would eliminate intermediate-range nuclear missiles. Reagan declared war against international terrorism. He commanded naval escorts in the Persian Gulf, and maintained the free flow of oil during the Iran-Iraq war. In keeping with the Reagan Doctrine, he gave support to anti-Communist insurgencies in Central America, Asia, and Africa.

Though Pete usually votes Democratically, he really favored President Reagan. During a dialogue on the job one day, Pete was conversing with a young man from New York when he revealed how much he respected and liked Mr. Reagan. "You're a Black man and likes President Reagan?" He fired back, "Of course I like him and think he's a very strong and positive man, and President."

Even in the 80s, President Reagan envisioned implementing Star Wars, which caused for interceptors/or missiles to shot down incoming missiles from rogue countries. Pete applauded this concept. Mr. Reagan is the one who vociferously said to Mr. Gorbachev, "Tear down that wall!" Referring to the Berlin Wall. It brought forth historical significance and precedence during the aftermath of its demolition. During his administration, how could anyone forget that he dubbed the Soviet Union, as an 'Evil Empire.'

Just after he was sworn into office, Iran released the American hostages who were held in captivity for about one year. The reporter, who was believed Sam Donaldson, apprised immediately after he was sown into office, "Mr. President, the hostages have been freed." Because of throng surrounding him, he inquired, "Say what?" Sam Donaldson spoke a little louder a second time. With a broader than life grin on his face, he offered, "Good."

Because of his theatrical film roles, and a suspected, don't-take-any-stuff-attitude, he said shortly after his inauguration, "Well, they call me a trigger-happy westerner, but I haven't fired the first shot."

Now turning to President Clinton. During the administration of William Jefferson Clinton, the U.S. enjoyed more peace and economic well being than at any other time in history. He was the first Democratic President since Franklin D. Roosevelt to win a second term. He could point to the lowest unemployment rates in modern times, the lowest inflation in 30 years, the highest home ownership in the country's history, dropping crime rates in many places, and reduced welfare roles. He proposed the first balanced budget in decades and achieved a budget surplus. As part of a plan to celebrate the millennium in 2000, Clinton called for a great national initiative to end racial discrimination.

After the failure in his second year of a huge program of health care reform, Clinton shifted emphasis, declaring "the era of big government is over." He sought legislation to upgrade education, to protect jobs of parents who care for sick children, to restrict hand gun sales, and to strengthen environmental rules.

President Clinton, born William Jefferson Blythe IV on August 19, 1946, in Hope, Arkansas, three months after his father died in a traffic accident. When he was four years old, his mother married Roger Clinton, of Hot Spring, Arkansas. In high school, he took the family name.

He excelled as a student and as a saxophone player and once considered becoming a professional musician. As a delegate to Boys Nation while in high school, he met President John Kennedy in the White House Rose Garden. The run-in led him to enter a life of public service.

Clinton graduated from Georgetown University and in 1968, won a Rhodes scholarship to Oxford University. He received a law degree from Yale University in 1973, and entered politics in Arkansas.

He was defeated in his campaign for Congress in Arkansas's Third District in 1974. The next year he married Hillary Rodham, a graduate of Wellesley College and Yale Law School. In 1980, Chelsea, their only child, was born.

Clinton was elected Arkansas Attorney General in 1976, and won the governorship in 1978. After losing a bid for a second term, he regained the office four years later, and served until he defeated incumbent George Bush and third party candidate Ross Perot in the 1992 presidential race.

Clinton and his running mate, Tennessee's Senator Albert Gore Jr., then 44, represented a new generation in American Political leadership. For the first time in 12 years both the White House and Congress were held by the same party. But that political edge was brief; the Republicans won both houses of Congress in 1994.

In 1998, as a result of issues surrounding personal indiscretions with a young female White House intern, Clinton was the second U.S. president to be impeached by the House of Representatives. He was tried in the Senate and found not guilty of the charges brought against him. He apologized to the nation for his actions and continued to have unprecedented popular approval ratings for his job as President.

He successfully dispatched peace keeping forces to war-torn Bosnia and bombed Iraq when Saddam Hussein stopped United Nations inspections for evidence of nuclear, chemical, and biological weapons. He became a global proponent for an expanded NATO, opened more international trade, and was a worldwide campaign against drug trafficking. He drew huge crowds when he traveled through South America, Europe, Russia, Africa, and China, advocating U.S. style freedom.

Of all the listed presidents, Pete favored President Clinton the most based on his credentials, intelligence and productions. This was not to say Mr. Clinton was a better president than John F. Kennedy, because he deemed John F. Kennedy a paragon. Too bad his administration was cut short by a crazed assassin.

President Clinton was well-liked by everyone due primarily to his executed policies and agendas. To mull over the fact he was the second Democratic president since Franklin D. Roosevelt to win a second term in office, tells that he was the people's choice. During the time he was attacked by Republicans for what he called an inappropriate relationship with an intern. Fannie, Pete's mother always said, "Why don't they leave him along, as good-looking as he is, women are going to want him. He just got weak and made a mistake...They should just forgive him."

Pete's perspective was similar to Fannie's. But what he did wasn't right or moral, yet he shouldn't have been impeached and persecuted for something that's venial. Sure, many individuals say he lied about his relationship with the intern and wasn't forthright about it. As Christian practices, one should never advocate mendacity but always posture to tell the truth and be forthright. When it becomes something as sacred and private as an intimate relationship. Most individuals are reticent and secretive, therefore, Mr. Clinton's initial reaction was understandable. This does not mean that adultery is right and should be practiced, but rather, when a man and woman agree to marriage, each one makes a covenant and commitment, saying no to any other man or woman in the world. No exception!

When gays wanted to serve in the military where there was known abuse once a person revealed his or her sexual persuasion, the President was shrewd enough to develop the policy "Don't Ask, Don't Tell." Pete applauded this policy, saving face with everyone and appeasing the gay community and averting psychological and physical abuse.

Most notably, he's credited with enabling Americans to enjoy the lowest unemployment rate in modern times, the lowest inflation rate in 30 years, the highest home ownership in the country's history, reduced crime rate in many locales and reduced welfare roles. Moreover, he proposed the first balanced budget in decades, as well as a budget surplus.

Mr. Clinton credited his vice president Al Gore for much, especially regarding balancing the budget. Plus, he credits his wife, the former first lady, for any measurement of success during his administration.

Despite his one indiscretion while in office, if he could have run for president a third term, he would probably still be President of the United States. He sure would have gotten Pete's vote, and presumably many others. In fact, Pete longed for the time when the Constitution would change, allowing for a third term in office. Sage knowledge has it that, today, the United States would probably be in better condition if the Constitution allowed three terms.

Comparing Clinton's presidency to John F. Kennedy, President Kennedy and first lady, Mrs. Kennedy had high standards by which others are mentioned and compared, displaying personableness, grace and charisma. President Clinton, like J.F.K., was highly intelligent, personable, and did a wonderful job during his tenure. Both first ladies were charming, beautiful and intelligent. Therefore, if Mrs. Hillary Clinton can win the democratic nomination, she, no doubt, will be the very first woman president, and will surely get Pete's vote and the community of individuals who want change and a better direction.

Nine

Geographical Transition

OHN TRANSFERRED FROM HAMILTON HIGH School to Trinity High School during his tenth year of schooling along with Pete. This change naturally caused Sally to transfer to Trinity also. Having graduated from Trinity High School, rather than Hamilton, they both agreed that it was a very positive change. Although they graduated from Trinity, the actual structure was The Decatur High School campus, where the actual graduation and commencement activities took place.

Residing in Washington Park and attending Trinity wasn't in accord with legal districting at the time. Sally and Pete claimed to live with a lady by the name of Odessa. When the system cracked down on students living out of the proper district, John had to leave Trinity at the beginning of his twelfth school year, and eventually attended Murphy High School, and would graduate from there. Obviously Pete was saddened over John's ouster.

Shortly following the death of their father, Hayman, on July 6, 1973, Sally met a Floridian young man whom she married, they moved to California in the mid 70s. The marriage didn't set well with Pete, Buck and mother, Fannie. Sally boasted having been a virgin at age 23, and it certainly wasn't doubted when considering all she would do, studying incessantly. Realistically, any male suitors whom she would see had to be scrutinized by Pete and Buck, whether she accepted their perspectives and opinions, they were sternly given just the same. It was concern and care, born from pure love that they had for her. As late as the 90s, a suitor who stood about 6 ft 5' came to see her. Buck questioned, "Pete, what do you think about those polyester slacks he was wearing?" "Not much," Pete answered.

Oscar, her husband, was no different, they opposed the marriage, including Fannie. A tell-tell sign that the marriage was doomed from the start, was when Sally drove from California to Georgia twice, either because of something he did or some tiff.

Pete, on September 25, 1983, moved to Los Angeles, California and lived with Sally, Fannie and Oscar temporarily. Immediately following kissing and embracing Fannie, he asked for water to drink and quickly exclaimed, "What's wrong with this water, it tastes like medicine?" "We have to boil our water, because it does taste a little funny," Sally responded.

Pete immediately liked LA and thought it vastly different from Georgia, but admittedly, thought by and large, people from Georgia were more friendly. He was amused by the massive, but diverse composition of races and liked what he saw. Additionally, he was impressed by Mayor, Mr. Tom Bradley whom he deemed a fair, kind and impartial person.

Pete would befriend and worked for Harry doing part-time work as a custodian maintenance man and worked part-time at Hughes. Harry was the brother-in-law to an all-star pro football player who played for the Oakland/Los Angeles Raiders. Obviously Pete attended many Los Angeles Raiders' home games and enjoyed himself immensely.

Pete loved most sports and played softball. Baseball and basketball may have been his favorites, he loved baseball, watching the first inning to the last inning. His favorite teams were the Atlanta Braves and the Los Angeles Angels. His favorite broadcasters were, Vince Scully, Skip Carey, Joe Morgan and John Miller. In promoting mental happiness, Pete advocated preoccupying himself doing things he liked. Even psychologists make mention that a person lives longer when his mind is happy...And when one lavishes in humor, it erases many ills and converts them into thrills and exhilaration.

After finishing a Telecommunication course, Pete started working full-time at a student loan finance company as an Office Coordinator, a job created and given to him by the vice-president of the company, principally due to his written and verbal skills. Ironically, that particular company, was the one that provided a loan grant for his Telecommunication course.

The student loan company, admittedly, was a friendly, family-oriented place that attracted some of the finest employees anyone could ever want to meet. Three of his good friends to-date once worked for the company; more noteworthy, his long-time lady friend, to whom he befriended during the mid 80s worked there.

Many of the former student loan employees still play softball to-date. Pete, as a pitcher, started playing softball in 1986, on a team called the Artesian. His best friend Ray, relieved the pitching chores from the vice-president, and assigned the starting pitching to Pete. Interestingly enough, in the very first season for Pete, the Artesian's won the championship. Ray, who was a true competitor but a bit temperamental, hated losing and at times became irascible. Before the two bonded, Pete hollered at one of his teammates encouraging him to run to an advance base. "Why are you telling him to run when you can't run," Ray reasoned. Rather than become affected,

Pete immediately mulled over what was said and reasoned to himself: He's not lying because he had always been slow.

During the championship game, which was at Wilson Park and was attended by Pete's mother and sister, Sally, after the game would ask, "Why does he (Ray) get on you like that?" "He doesn't mean any harm, he just knows at times I'll screw up," Pete replied laughingly.

Three years later, while still working at this student loan company, Pete would write published articles in its monthly Newsletter. He wrote the following pertaining to their softball team:

March 1, 1989

Support Your Local Softball Team

Our season opener started off with a bang...or better yet, a TKO (technical knockout.)

To begin with, I had sustained a hyper-extended right arm via a workout with weights. Excruciating pain was felt from my lower arm to my right shoulder each time I threw the ball. As a pitcher, this spelled bad news for my teammates.

How did I feel about going into their first game of the season? Pessimistic. Confirmation came later when I found out we had but eight players. It takes ten players to constitute a team, but the league will permit play with eight players (less than eight and the game cannot be played.)

The ultimate confirmation of my pessimism came during the second inning while the opposing team was at the plate. Someone hit a pop fly, this sent Ray and Kent scurrying to make the catch. At full speed, they collided! Ray was knocked out and Kent (who suffered a broken wrist and a dislocated thumb) lay there in obvious pain. Not realizing he was unconscious, I stood over Ray saying, "Ray, are you okay?" Seconds later he awoke and acknowledged that he was "Fine." I breathed a sigh of relief and attended to Kent. William, Ray's supervisor over Accounting, came over to me and said, "Pete, it's Ray who is messed up...he doesn't know where he is." Pete went to Ray's side and inquired, "Ray, are you okay?" He replied, "Yes." So Pete proceeded to ask, "Who is the president of the United States?" Ray looked at him ruefully and answered, "Reagan." Pete insisted, "You guys take him home." They laughed uncontrollably. At the time of the collision, the score was 3-4 favoring the opposing team. This was the final score as their team needed two more players to continue the game.

By: Pete

Ray actually lost two months of memory, and even asked one of his teammates to tell his girlfriend, Suzette, about his incident. Someone said, "You don't go with her anymore, your current girlfriend is Grace."

Meanwhile, at the student loan Finance Co., everyone stood on tip-toe excitement regarding the annual, Summer Softball Play during their picnic. D.P. Data Processing had been the reigning champions for two straight seasons. Until Pete in his very first year, along with his Artesians teammates, won the championship, 1986. Rumor circulated throughout the company that he was a good pitcher, evoking comparison of Orel Hershiser of the Dodgers. People hurled out suggestions, calling him the "Bull Dog." Even further, he was called Bob Gibson, and therefore, D.P. felt threatened to relinquish their crown to Central Services, where Pete worked as an Office Coordinator.

During the company picnic, it was a nip and tuck affair, and at the off-set, it looked as if Central Services would win the coveted championship. Pete was confounded and puzzled by this one young man on the D.P.'s squad. The arch of the pitch was unlimited, and Pete was so precise, he could seemingly land his pitch on a dime after lofting many pitches over 15 ft. in height.

The regular height is between 10-12 feet. Regardless of how high or the location of landing the pitch on any part of the plate, Spencer would hit majestic shots out of the park. Central Services was leading in late innings but wasn't able to contain Data Processing, thanks to a torrid-hitting Spencer, whose team won by one run. When it was all over, Pete's companion said, "That team (D.P.) didn't beat you, he did, referring to Spencer. Pete, immediately started admiring Spencer's hitting ability, and eventually his fine qualities as a man; someone whom he calls his friend. Spencer still plays on their softball team to-date.

The composition of their team was a mixture of Latinos, Blacks but predominantly Whites. One day while playing, Spencer overheard a Black guy on an opposing team say something racist, and Spencer quickly related it to Pete. "We don't need any of that, especially in a modern world as we know it," replied Pete.

This student loan company attracted and galvanized fine individuals. For instance, Spencer would meet and marry a young lady who worked for the company. She was attractive, kind, intelligent and forthright. Besides Ray, Andre', whom Pete dubbed, "The Giant," due to his 6ft 6 frame, is also his best friend. Like Spencer, he too would meet and marry a young, attractive lady who worked at the company.

Marriage is sacred and very personal and requires serious scrutiny before undertaking. Although Pete never married and had no children, but by his own admission, the only two women he likely would have married is his ex-girlfriend from Atlanta, GA, and his lady friend whom he met at the student loan company. Obviously Pete prefers marriage over bachelorhood living, but if it never happens, he'll continue to live happily and contentedly. Just recently a female inquired, "Say you never been married and have no children, how anyone let you get away?" He replies, "Marriage is something I'd like to be, but not begging to be."

Misogamist? No! Pete isn't. Rather, mental maturity and vying the life of a Christian. Unlike his life during his late teens and early 20s where indiscretion ran rampant, becoming the norm and not the rule, now he refuses to yield to indiscretion and reprobate characteristics.

"This life is completely different. This I say then, walk in the Spirit, and ye shall not fulfill the lust of the flesh," Galatians, Chapter 5, Verse 16. While perfection is pervasive in all individuals, but self-control should become a common practice by everyone. Paul, in I Corinthians, Chapter 7, Verse 9, is curt and clear, reading, "But if they cannot contain, let them marry: for it is better to marry than to burn." (Burn with passion) In the same Chapter, Verse 32 and 33 read: "But I would have you without carefulness. He that is unmarried careth for the things that belong to the Lord, how he may please the Lord: But he that is married careth for the things that are of the world, how he may please his wife."

Sometimes couples marry too young and know very little about each other's traits, mind-set, emotions and general make-up. By the time all is ascertained, the couple is headed towards split-ville. Pete recalled during his last year of high school when he had begun a relationship with this young lady who was in the eleventh grade. No one could tell him the affair wasn't substantial and he didn't love her. Empiricism declares the temporary courtship preliminary, lacks merits. Unfortunately, this lady passed away recently in 2007. She was a very nice and good person, and was rooted strongly into Christianity. Regarding marriage, Pete felt couples should know each other for at least two years and sometimes longer to even consider such a union.

Recently while listening to a Sunday morning gospel radio station, a pastor asked God to send him a mate. He met a young lady from some club who was described by him as beautiful and fine. Following about 3 months of courtship this lady's pattern would stay the same, whereas she frequented clubbing. The pastor would say to God, I think she's the one, maybe I can change her from wanting to go clubbing. Admittedly, he would say, the harder he tried to dissuade her the more she wanted to go. The moral of the story, he concluded, "When I said yes, God was saying no, dummy."

An allegory but true in nature: One could take 150 individuals living in the ghetto and place them in a section of Beverly Hills, CA, and shortly afterwards, the section in which they live would look like the ghetto. Yes, the ghetto is lodged within the individual; conversely, clubbing was lodged within this particular woman.

Regarding the student loan company, Mr. Kemp, who was the founder and CEO of the company, got lofty commendations for helping individuals, like Pete to acquire higher learning. He displayed a picture-perfect epitome of forthrightness, integrity, honesty and impartiality. He looked down on no one and treated everyone fairly and equally and at the same time, exhibited class and a stature of respectability. He allowed people an opportunity to show their worth. After all, if a person isn't given a chance to fail, then it is impossible to succeed.

His staff reflected his image, especially in administration, including his vice-president and Human Resource Specialist. Vice-president, Dan was a nice, caring compassionate person who also gave his subordinates a chance to show and prove their worth. Not only did he play softball with his Artesian teammates but would host parties at his home with his employees who then, resided in Palo Verdes, CA. They played music, games and would swim in his personal swimming pool. Regarding the Human Resource Specialist, Reese, her beauty ran parallel to her shrewdness and intellect. Pete, of course, would befriend her and would learn many positive things from her; particularly, always staying positive even when the walls are cracking, knowing danger is imminent.

During a dialogue with Reese at lunch one day, Pete, whose interest was piqued by a young Filipina, would ask Reese her perspectives on Filipinos. She would articulate "They are sincere and dedicated workers and, on the most part, don't cross over dating out of their race. But frankly, I suggest an American woman for you." Pete appreciated her candor and advice. Obviously she had seen him going to lunch with Peggy and envisioned them as an interesting couple with a ton of commonalties.

Pete really did appreciate Dan, who created the employment position in Central Services and awarded it to him. He immediately liked and admired his supervisor, Sharon. She imparted the work production and performance of one's subordinates. Referring to the employee whom Pete was in charge. "Develop tough skin," she insisted many a time. Never will Pete forget what she would say whenever a person was about to leave the company who was a thorn in the side, she'd say, "How can I miss you when you won't go away?"

Every Monday morning Pete would have to do inventory of the stocks, a chore he dreaded doing vehemently — inventory of reams of paper to post-it-notes, invoices, etc. Obviously he knew the reason for doing it but just couldn't reason with it and non-surprisingly, his inventory count was never accurate. Whenever the chore was designated to someone else and that person's inventory count was incorrect, Sharon would be furious and would say, "Anybody who can't simply count and, gets the inventory wrong, I don't need them." "But I always come up incorrect," Pete offered. "Yeah, but that's you," she rendered smilingly.

Pete was happy when the company hired Keith in his department. Principally because he would be given the opportunity to do inventory. Not once did he louse up the inventory count. Keith had a very calm demeanor and a grand personality and was extremely meticulous in performing all of his responsibilities. Inevitably, they became good friends. Usually when Pete was being paged and wouldn't answer, Keith knew where he was, he would always be in Peggy's office. To-date, they laughed about it. Pete was honored to partake in Keith's wedding in San Diego, 1988.

At this church, they had rehearsed with everyone in place except the groom, and when he showed up, Pete inquired, "What took you so long to show up?" Pete would ask.

"I was just riding around in the limousine drinking and just thinking about things,' he confided with a smile.

"Shuck, that is something to think about," referring to marriage.

Keith married a very nice young lady from San Diego, and to-date, they're residing in Houston, Texas, working for his father who is an entrepreneur. When seeking true friendship, especially teenagers, listen to a person's conversation and follow his actions very closely, action is a blue-print of the heart. Oftentimes, everything that's spoken is in stark contrast to what the mind contains. Additionally, many spoken words through the teeth do not exist in the heart; rather, the continuation of a person's action, judges the heart.

Pete embraced the friendship with John based on his parental upbringing and his good character. As a life-long friend, Pete weighed in on what John had to say and saw action in motion as very good. Too many teens are too quick to claim friendship where proper time isn't given to determining a person's true nature. A person who lies a lot is not born of goodness and becomes not only a deceiver to others but a true detriment to himself. Residing in a more high-tech, sophisticated, computerized society where everything is at your finger-tip, young people are drowning in the morass of sin and lasciviousness, primarily due to being influenced by bad company. All things considered, one could live a life-time with true friendship consisting of a handful of people. However, when a person can truly count more than a handful of friends over a life-time, attribute it to God. Credit God for placing these people in your sphere of existence and yourself for your ability to attract reputable individuals. If the cliché is true, unalike attracts, then alikeness must be truly multiplied.

Keith and Pete, though far apart, are still good friends.

A brief spot-light on John, Pete's life-long best friend, a friendship was begun just prior to the first grade of school. To say he is a successful entrepreneur would be an under statement. John, besides being a proprietor of a Day Care Center and owner of a Brake and Automotive Repair Shop, recently sold his package store and sold-out his service station to East Lake Country Club, a golf course.

John is the President of Anglers Paradise Fishing Club. He appeared on a local Atlanta T.V. network show, hosting and promoting his fishing club. Anglers Paradise was hosted by John for about two years from 2001-2002. He is probably the only Black-American to host such a program.

Ray was befriended by Pete mainly because of his proclivity to help others. He displayed a fine personality. While working at the student loan company, occasionally employees would inadvertently lock their keys in their cars. He became adapt at getting into their cars with a slim-jim-like object. He showed Pete how to open locked cars. Early one summer morning in 1987, a young lady at work, inadvertently locked her keys in her truck, the engine was running with her baby inside. Pete came to her rescue. People looking on had begun to panic, Pete stayed calm but steadfast in prayer. Within 5 minutes the door became unlocked. Pete silently prayed, "Thank you Dear Heavenly Father." Then he thought about how Ray had taught him to unlock cars and thanked Ray too.

Coincidentally, Ray and Pete owned a Pinto automobile during the early to mid 80s. Pete's supervisor charged, "I should have your and Ray's cars towed away from the parking lot for littering," a smiling Sharon offered. After arriving to work simultaneously and parking near each other, Pete suggested to Peggy, "Do you want me to take you to lunch today?" "No! That's okay, your car makes too much noise," Peggy replied.

Shortly thereafter, Pete purchased two additional cars, and when Ray's Pinto engine threw a rod, Pete practically gave him his Pinto, for $50.00.

Just prior to that transaction, Ray, one night was working on his Pinto, trying to remove its transmission during nightfall when a policeman admonished him from a helicopter hovering above, saying, "All right, crawl away from under the car and raise your arms and hand above your head." Once Ray did so, there were ground cops with guns drawn. Ray would immediately explain: "Sir, this is my car, why would anyone want to steel any thing like this?" After verifying it was his car, the cops disclosed someone reported someone was possibly trying to steal a car.

After working for over a year in Central Services, Pete applied for and was granted a transfer to D.P. (Data Processing), and given the title, inventory clerk. Besides doing inventory, he ran 25 pair cabling, wired 66 M blocks, and would wire up computers and terminals. This was an assignment which was more in alignment with his completed course in Telecommunications. During this particular stint, he would meet and befriend Andre', who, like Ray, would become his very good friend. While Pete did most of the hardware side of telecommunications, Andre' would do the software aspects, by programming things.

Pete immediate supervisor was Montel, who heralded from Maine. Admittedly, he was extremely knowledgeable in telecommunications, but lacked inner-personal skills and was also a bit bias. There were some things he supposedly wanted Pete to learn but would impart it in a I-know-you-won't-get-it-due-to-my-superficial-description. Ironically, Pete did learn to do everything required of him. Montel just blurted out to Pete, "I'm from Main, and I never met a Black person there that I liked." What did Pete say to that? He was mum and clearly read him as bias and shallow-minded. What is racial hatred or prejudice but a gangrene plagued individual with a mentality so overwhelmed with rubbish and cancer that eventually and inevitably it will consume that individual.

There was a young White lady who worked in Collections who liked Montel. A somewhat full-figured Black young lady also worked in Collections, asked Pete to relate to Montel that Renee likes him. Before he could tell Montel, J.J., the Black lady approached Montel, asking, "Montel, do you have a girlfriend?" "No! And I'm not looking for one." Of course, J.J.would approach Pete to say Montel was prejudiced, something he already knew, but, like always, trying to save face, Pete assured her that he wasn't, assuming he thought the interesting party was J.J. In actuality, Montel was prejudiced, based on things he would say and do, because a person's actions judges the heart.

Having worked under Montel for about one year, he gave Pete extremely low evaluations, thus, small raises in salary. There was one instance when a staff's terminal was not working properly and Pete did trouble-shooting and found it at the time working. He got the proper person to sign the work order sheet but later the terminal reverted to its bad functioning. Montel went to check it out doing basically the same thing Pete did, and said, "It's okay; now. He told the staffer to never sign off on any thing Pete does." This infuriated Pete who would go to Montel's supervisor to inform what Montel said to this staffer. Mr. Moore, his supervisor, impugned him, saying, never do that again in front of an employee. Montel apologized to Pete and said he was only kidding and would find out there was a bad circuit component within the Computer Room causing the terminal to not function properly.

Eventually, the evaluations got lower until Montel wanted to transfer Pete to another department. In conjunction with the low grading, purporting Pete didn't finish work orders in a timely manner, plus his work was shoddy. Within his rebuttal letter, Pete challenged that if his work was shoddy and he didn't finish work orders in a timely manner, where was the written warning? Pete shared a copy of his rebuttal letter with the Human Resource Specialist, Reese, who said, "You got a point, it's up to you to take any action." Rather than get transferred to another department, Pete elected to resign and devoted time to self-employment, but did warn a colleague, who was a Black female, to watch out and be aware of Montel. A very good friend who worked there advised Pete to sue the company, but Pete didn't want to because of his loyalty and respect for the CEO and Vice-President. True to suspicion, Montel got rid of Pete's former colleague. Speculatively, Montel's action piqued higher authority which drew drastic changes. Montel was stripped of his supervisory position and would later resign from the company.

Andre' cautioned, "Pete, you could do and did your job requirements, it was just Montel, and I can't stand him." Montel played on the softball team for a period. Obviously Pete conveyed to Buck, his brother, the conduct of Montel's, attitude and bias. Buck usually visited Pete once a year from Atlanta, GA to LA. On one particular Saturday morning, 1989, when Pete and Buck had just parked in the ball-park for a softball game, Montel swiftly and carelessly parked next to them on the passenger side. Though Buck had never seen him but perceptibly suggested, "That's that red-neck, isn't it?" "How did you know?" "That just got to be him, had I opened my door he would have hit me," Buck reasoned.

LA is known for its many quips and slogans. There was a bumper sticker that read: "Mean People Suck." For every deep rooted prejudiced and racial hatred individuals, there should be a slogan to read: "A gangrene plagued individual with racial hatred is bonafide dung and should be flushed immediately."

The development of prejudice in many cases is inherited, practiced by offspring's and lynch-mob mentalities that preceded us. And some individuals live illusionary lives, thinking they're better than the next person or race. Actuality teaches: It is good to subscribe to self-esteem, but once it becomes excessive, it replaces self-centeredness — and we know such a pride chokes the sense out of reality. While serving a forgiving God and residing in a forgiving society with respect to past prejudices and atrocities, sure it irks us once a bad tare crops up among us rearing its ugly head. It's good, however to remember, to never be perturbed by the mentally disturbed, otherwise, we will become tilt.

Reflection of a Friendship

SINCE AROUND 1985, RAY AND Pete have been best of friends, having met at the student loan company. What really brought them close was Ray's propensity to help fellow staffers at their workplace. There were incidents where some workmates would lock the keys in their cars. Ray was adept at getting into their cars, retrieving their keys in a short time. Pete would learn to do likewise by watching him perform his skills. Helping others has been in Pete's make-up ever since his memory can recall, and seeing how Ray would go out the way to assist fellow workmates, made Pete inwardly affirm, "He's my kind of people." Pete definitely doesn't quickly embrace the notion of true friends within a short span of time. Realistically, time is the truest barometer in determining true friends. It will make you or break you. But to acknowledge friendship, no one anywhere could ever have a truer friend; someone who can be relied upon until the end; someone who stands ever-ready to perform a deed or service without boasting what was done and when it was done. He once described a friend: "A person upon whom one can depend and someone who does not keep a record of who did the last deed; rather, someone akin to a brother who knows the other strengths and weaknesses and would never proclaim or exploit them." Undeniably, prior to the acquisition of friendship, one has to gamble at the risk of trust before claiming a friend. And when the occasion of inconvenience arises, simultaneously, when one asks a favor, it should be done immediately and pleasingly.

Over twenty years of friendship, the given qualifications have been quantified, qualified and certified, establishing indestructible and perpetual friendship.

Ray once said his friends were Pete's friends, an assertion later in life that proved ever so true, glistening with much merits.

Ray would leave the company around 1988, and was hired at USC as a Bookkeeper, performing account receivables and payable tasks. His supervisor was a swell young lady who epitomizes unbiasness impartiality, affableness, kindness and decency. With candor, Pete inquired about the qualifications required to acquire the job position Ray landed. "Quite simple, just someone who can figure, add, divide and subtract accurately. Some applicants were so slow using the calculator when taking the test, and were so questionable, while Ray calculated accurately and quickly in his head, and didn't use the calculator," she offered. Louise, Ray's supervisor, used to play softball on the co-ed team. Since she batted left-handed, Pete dubbed her lefty and boasts she was a very good hitter. She became a friend of Pete's.

From the student loan company, Pete befriended other friends, meeting his long-time 'pinay' there in 1987. While working in Central Services as an office coordinator, he befriended Keith, who too, worked in his department. Pete was most proud when Keith asked him to be a participant in his wedding in San Diego in 1988. His wife resided there. Keith and his family moved to Houston, TX. A friendship that is still solid. Pete would change departments, becoming employed in Data Processing where he befriended Andre. In fact, like Ray, he qualifies Andre' his best friend. To acknowledge best friends, there are unquestionable qualifications and unfettered love that's inexplicable. Also, Pete was a friend to Kyra, his pinay's best friend. When she and James got married in 1987, Pete's mom would be the one who would be the power and crowning adult to give Kyra away in marriage. When looking over the wedding photos, many inquirers wanted to know was she a Filipina due to Fannie's fair complexion. Pete and Peggy are still friends, a friendship formulated in 1983. Spencer remains too, a solid friend.

Meanwhile, since 1986, Pete and friends, some of whom, once worked at the student loan company, still enjoy softball play. Just the camaraderie was spiritually uplifting. How much longer will the softball team play continue was anyone's guess. To-date, the play had spanned 21 years –1986-2007. The team hasn't stood too frequently in the winning circle, but May 8, 2007, the team had to win its last two games after winning about two during the spring league play. Fortunately, they won not only the two games to make the play-off, but won the entire play-offs, bringing euphoria and exhilaration to everyone on the team. It was a feeling of intoxication and jubilation on May 8, 2007. And unlike the previous season, the team had tasted defeat just once during the summer league play. Everyone likes each other on the team; they win together and lose together. During many games, there was always one ball-player having a great game, someone laud, "John Doe deserves the most valuable player." Ray exclaimed, "We're all valuable players."

The make up of the team varied from time to time, age-wise, 19 to 50, predominantly White, two American-Blacks, and Latinos. One player has an intriguing background, Lance's father was Puerto Ricans and mother was Somaliland. Like everyone on the team, this young man was charismatic and personable. It would be remissed not to mention William who played on the team and is still employed at the student loan company. He is Mexican-American, one of the kindest people anyone would be proud to call a friend. His wife was a reflection of himself and not to mention their two sons who are so handsome and precious. Each time they attend a game they'd say, "Hey Pete!" And they would extend their hands for good luck. Obviously, they made Pete reflect, if not regret on not having off-springs, thinking what could have been or should have been.

Pete would meet Kathy and befriended her, she was extremely beautiful with such radiant personality and demeanor. The copious conversations exchanged cemented their friendship from the mid 90s. Kathy expressed a deep love regarding her fiancé, describing what a wonderful person he was. Pete was most honored to be invited to their wedding in 2004.They are an amorous and amicable couple. Joseph, the husband, was introduced to Pete's friends, and now is a member of their fraternity. He is considered a true friend of Pete's. How could Pete forget when Andre' loss his mother when he asked what could he do to help? "Just get friendly faces there," Andre' suggested. Ironically, some of their fraternity clan who had known him for years didn't show up, but there stood Joseph, Ray and some others close friends.

Ray is the coach-player of their softball team, plus the main leader of the pact. While profiling him, he is a good person, though temperamental but good-natured nevertheless. Never will memory fade when one Sunday while playing on a co-ed team in Torrance, CA, the opposing team didn't have enough players and the game was forfeit. There were those two little boys wanting to shag some fly balls when Pete said, "Yeah, go out into the outfield, we'll hit you some balls." Someone suggested on Pete's team, "Come on, lets go to a pizza parlor." During their preparation to leave, this male, apparently the father of the boys, got somewhat close to Pete with an angry voice, exclaiming, "What do you mean, Pete, telling my boys to go out into the field and you're not going to hit balls to them?" Ray's eyes open wide like he's waiting for Pete to deck this guy.

Pete's philosophy had always been, "Fighting casts the reflection of a foolish act and should be engaged under only inevitable circumstances."

Therefore Pete undauntedly turned towards the little boys in the outfield, yelling, "I'm sorry, my team has to go." This defused potential hostility.

Reflecting on skirmishes between their softball team and others, such flare-ups had been sporadically seldom. Many years ago, Troy, a Latino and former teammate would love to fight and when doing so, it brought two teams together shoving and hollering.

In 1993, while vacationing in Atlanta, GA, Pete received a disheartening call from Ray's then-girlfriend who was a pathologist, to reveal Ray sustained a broken neck. Ray and his roommate went to Palms Springs with Ray diving into the water to swim, thinking he was diving in a deep level of water, he dove in the shadow, hitting his head on the ground. Consequently, he had to wear a complete head and neck gear with screws and torque fittings for about six months. Driving Ray on errands, occasionally, he drew chuckles from onlookers which infuriated Pete.

Ironically, less than six months of the neck brace removal, Ray was back on the softball field playing his regular first base position. On one occasion he and another player collided as Pete looked on in consternation.

Inwardly, Pete was overly concerned with the idea of him re-injuring his neck, realizing the possibility of paralysis or sudden death could occur from any violent impact. But it never occurred. Once Ray who is 6 feet 2 inches, weighing then around 220 lbs., got into a brief scuffle with an opposing team-player with the antagonist weighing a little more than Ray and about an inch or so taller. This occurred about a month or so following the removal of his neck support apparatus. When Pete observed what was happening, he saw both participants rolling on the ground as Pete scurried to the rescue, yelling, "Break it up!"

Ray would later confirm that this guy put a head-lock on him trying to choke him. Had Pete seen such action, his response to pry them apart would have been instantaneous. Everything turned out all right; no injury or extracurricular activity ensued.

Pete usually utilizes diplomacy and tact when pushing and shoving breaks out, knowing the three key components that prevent world war are: compromise, concession and restraint.

CHAPTER
Eleven

Turbulence in LA

ESIDING IN CALIFORNIA, THERE IS always something going on besides Oscar nominations, award galas, movies debuts, NBA celebrations by the Lakers, the Dodgers winning the World Series in 1988, or with the Lakers winning the NBA Championship the same year. The Angels won the World Series in 2002. Angelinos are accustomed to brush fires and earthquakes. The last sizable quake occurred in January, 1994, which frayed the nerves of inhabitants — with many individuals leaving LA permanently.

Exceeding the turbulence of the earthquake in 1994, was the video beating of Rodney King by the Simi Valley policemen in 1991. This blatant police brutality shook the very foundation of LA, and sent many business establishments up in smoke. As the smolder lingered, so did tempers from Black-Americans. The beating scene had to be entrenched in the memory of anyone, anywhere in the world who had a T.V. Moreover, by Blacks, just the mere mention of the beating scene, emits electrical shock waves to dendrites of the brain.

Such misuse of police authority was a classic case in point, the more things change, the more they stay the same. Such barbarity was self-explanatory and self-hatred on the part of the LAPD. as their action was uncalled for and almost unforgivable. If a picture is worth more than a thousand words, the video taping shown so repetitiously over the T.V., was worth more than a million.

Then LA Chief of Police Daryl Gates responded to the beating saying it was only an aberration. This man was seriously despised by the Black community of LA. There were posters of his likeness posted throughout the community resembling a bulls-eye. Obviously his likeness was a mocked target, which psychologically and deeply ingrained in the minds of Blacks, good ridden. Such nonchalance of a response condoned and maybe endorsed the conduct of those policemen, and not to mention the so-called investigation that dragged on seemingly forever, producing no substantive consequences.

Emphasis was shifted to Rodney King as he was portrayed a criminal with a past record. At issue wasn't the character or make-up of Rodney King, rather, the senseless beating by rogue cops of an unarmed person. Such act would have been uncivil and uncalled for had the victim been a wild animal. What message does this barbaric scene sends to young children of policemen? Whispers around the community at the time by particularly young minorities, was that, cops were the worst gang members. In reality, the mass majority of policemen do not represent the uncivilized action in the Rodney King's case, only a minority. By Rodney King not stopping, some alleged that being kicked and beaten with billy clubs, was justifiable. Nonsense! Such action was flatly inexcusable.

Some years following the Rodney King saga, the Rampart LAPD Division became the focal point of scandal when Officer Rafael Perez disgraced himself, dishonoring his sworn pledge to serve and protect.

Such scandal revealed Perez and officer Nino Durden ran a drug-theft operation, planted evidence, framed suspects and lied in court.

The scandal cost taxpayers more than $72 million in payouts as 100 criminals' convictions were overturned. Despite the prevailing belief many additional officers were involved, just handfuls were charged. Moreover, it led to a costly federal court consent decree that brought the LAPD under the control of a federal monitor.

Obviously the senseless beating was a conversation-piece among Pete's circle of friends, all of whom were deemed deplorable. Some would theorize Rodney King's failure to stop probably infuriated the cops who lead to the beating with all agreeing though, was horrendous, inexcusable and reprehensible. This incidence preceded the Rampart saga where police misconduct became a revelation shocker. Such impropriety led to the release of some convicted persons due to corrupt cops, leading to enormous law suits by exonerated individuals. Within the Latino and Black community, to many, had encountered injustice by cops and thereby registered much mistrust and skepticism. Therefore, while watching the fiasco of Rodney King, speculatively, fortified mistrust Blacks and Latinos held towards cops. In fact, watching the horrific beating scene, was no shock at all; rather, a familiar refrain. Moreover, whenever an accumulation of mistreatments agitate the mind, it likely becomes akin to a build-up of volcanic lava, ready to blow at any moment.

The same notion triggered Rosa Parks after confronting racism, injustice and inhumanity for so long. Rationality is a clear teacher, for every action there is a reaction, and in the Rodney King's case, it was a delayed reaction. Such slow, so-called investigations by Daryl Gates didn't set well on the pulse of the Black community. The enormity of this civil rights violation brought about the Warren Commission that would look into the Department. And seemingly other Police Departments came under scrutiny in the U.S. in the wake of the King beating. Living in LA, one got the impression the entire world was watching to see how the incidence would unfold.

Sage practice is to be quick to observe, listen and learn but slow to judge. But in the King case, the million-like word video was similar to watching a horror flick over and over, seeing an assailant inflicting harm to the innocent. Aside from guilt, one reasons, how severe will the punishment be?

The criminal charge brought against those cops involving civil rights violation and police brutality brought even more shock to Angelinos and the country when a jury rendered a verdict of not guilty. While talking to Ray via phone during the reading of the verdicts, Pete apprised, "The first verdict was not guilty." "That's chicken s..t,!" Ray lamented. "Ain't nobody guilty," sighed Pete as the four not-guilty verdicts were announced. Sgt. Stacy Koon...Assault with a deadly weapon...Not guilty. Filing a false police report...Not guilty. Accessory after the fact...Not guilty.

Officer Laurence Powell...Assault with a deadly weapon...Not guilty. Excessive force under the color of authority...Dead-locked, mistrial declared. Filing a false police report...Not guilty.

Officer Theodore Briseno...Assault with a deadly weapon...Not guilty. Excessive force under the color of authority...Not guilty.

Officer Timothy Wind. Assault with a deadly weapon... Not guilty. Excessive force under the color of authority...Not guilty.

CHRONOLOGY

March 3, 1991: Lake View Terrace resident George Holliday uses video camera to record police beating motorist King after high-speed chase.

March 4: Videotape broadcast by Los Angeles television station KTLA, then shown nationwide by CNN and other stations.

March 6: Police Chief Daryl F. Gates apologizes for King's beating, but calls it an aberration. Critics call for his resignation.

March 7: King freed after prosecutors declined to file charges. Gates recommends prosecution for three officers in beating and pledges to discipline others.

March 15: Grand jury indicts Sgt. Stacey Koon and Officer Laurence Powell, Timothy Wind and Theodore Briseno. Charges include assault under the color of authority, assault with great bodily injury, excessive force and filing false police reports.

March 18: Communications transcript released in which officer in beating says he hadn't "beaten anyone this bad in a long time." Other messages: "Oops," "You just had a big time use of force," "I think he was dusted…many broken bones later…after the pursuit."

March 26: Indicted officers plead innocent.

March 27: Gates asks retired state Supreme Court Justice John Arguelles to head panel to examine excessive force incidents and recommend reforms.

March 30: Mayor Tom Bradley appoints former U.S. Deputy Secretary of State, Warren Christopher to head panel to investigate police practices.

April 4: Police Commission suspends Gates for 60 days. Arguelles and Christopher panels merge into single commission.

April 5: City council orders Gates reinstatement.

April 8: A Superior Court judge reinstates Gates.

May 7: Gates fires Wind and suspends Koon, Powell and Briseno without pay.

May 28: King allegedly tries to run over police officer after picking up a transvestite prostitute in Hollywood. Authorities decline to file charges, saying King believed officer was a civilian going to rob him.

July 9: Christopher Commission releases report citing evidence of brutality and racism in police force. It blamed deficient management, suggests that Gates retire and recommends imposing a term limit on future chiefs.

July 22: Gates says he'll retire in April 1992 if his replacement is chosen by then. He later postpones date to June, saying he wants to fight term limits and other reforms on June 2 city ballot.

Nov. 26: Superior Court Judge Stanley Weisberg orders trial held in Ventura County.

Feb. 5, 1992: Trial begins. Jury selection ends.

March 17: Prosecution rests without calling King to the stand.

April 16: Philadelphia Police Commissioner Willie Williams is introduced as Gates successor. Williams will be LAPD's first Black chief and first from outside the LAPD in more than 40 years.

April 20" Closing arguments begin King case.

April 23: Jury begins deliberations in King case.

April 29: Jury finds the four officers not guilty of assault and other charges except for a deadlock on the charge of excessive force against Powell in which four jurors voted for conviction and eight for acquittal. Weisberg orders a mistrial on the remaining charge against Powell, and orders the case returned to his court in Los Angeles for a May 15 hearing.

Scheduled next regarding the King case.

May 15, 1992, hearing in Los Angeles Superior Court on whether prosecutors will retry Officer Laurence Powell on an excessive force charge. The jury failed to reach a verdict on that count and a mistrial was declared.

❑   A federal civil right case filed by King.

❑   An 83 million claim against the City of Los Angeles filed by King.

❑   Administrative hearing for Sgt. Stacey Koon and officer Powell and Theodore Briseno to determine whether disciplinary action, including firing, should be taken. Timothy Wind, a rookie officer, was already granted a hearing and subsequently fired. He is seeking a second hearing.

Such incomprehensible verdicts sent shock waves of discontentment and discord throughout a nation of individuals, especially Angelinos. Even the U.S. Justice Department initiated a probe of the case, saying it would investigate the case of four current and former Los Angeles police officers acquitted of assault charges in last year's (1991) videotaped beating of Rodney King to determine whether civil rights laws were violated.

Fall-out from the verdict became a conversation-piece in many forms, including by members of the LAPD, despite Police Chief Daryl Gates' direction to police officers not to speak to reporters inside the police stations. Wednesday, April 29, 1991, a few spoke outside the Harbor Division.

The dedicated, conscience-driven officers offered: "The verdicts would be a small step toward restoring morale after a year of what many in uniform labeled "cop bashing." "It's going to take a lot more than this trial to bring up the level of morale in this department," Officer Robert Smith reasoned.

Shamefully, most police officers supported the accused officers.

"It's our brother out there who's going upon trial. We feel for him," said Officer Ben Warren. "They were found not guilty. They've been innocent all along." Additionally, "That's an extraordinary amount of stress to go through to be found not guilty," Warren said. "It will make us all think about what we are doing a little bit more. We've all learned from it."

Then there were officers who believed the accused used excessive force.

"While they were not convicted, the officers realize that not everything those officers did was good," said Capt. Timothy King, Harbor Division commander. "Things did not go well during that incident."

King worked in Internal Affairs and started the investigation of the four officers.

"I hate second guessing people, but doggone it, I did not like what I saw on the video," King said.

In the Black community it was sheer consternation at hearing, not guilty, not guilty, not guilty verdicts. The three color TVs in Sir Graham's Restaurant in Inglewood California, with the Breaking news, showed and videoed the not guilty verdicts.

"I feel a stab in the heart every time I hear that 'Not guilty,' said Ann Jackson as she watched one TV set from the bar.

"There really is no justice. This man was being kicked and beaten while he lay on the street."

"I started to cry," said bartender Cheryl Cornelous. "I expected some guilty verdicts, but not this. It's amazing."

"We (Blacks) don't amount to anything," she said. "We've been the lower class from slavery on. I didn't think they would get away with it because it was televised. They're saying, 'We don't give a damn about you.'"

Sir Graham Eatery is on La Brea Ave. And the mood there was solemn and mutual; the jury's verdicts were despicable and incomprehensible. The outcry and condemnation of the verdict was echoed in patron Marion Reid of Los Angeles, saying King was out numbered and never should have been severely beaten.

"There are some good police officers out there and there are bad ones." Reid said. "We wouldn't be walking out in the streets if we didn't have police. But those (accused Los Angeles officers are sadistic people) and they shouldn't be there. If there's a lot of violence (in the community following the verdict), it's that jury's fault."

Al Lang, a real estate developer, put things a little more in a realistic, philosophical perspective, saying the lesson of the King trial was important for younger Blacks who did not experience the flagrant racism of the 1950s and 1960s.

Today's young Blacks attend schools and make friends with Whites and don't understand racism is as much a part of American society as it was in the past, he said. "This is good. It will open their eyes to understand White folks at least as far as justice is concerned," he said.

Restaurant patron Byron Paul, who "claimed a lot of "street experience," offered an explanation for the mayhem violence that followed the verdict. "A lot of innocent people are going to get hurt because (young Blacks angered by the verdicts) can't get to the people they want. Black leaders are saying it's going to be all right."

Central complaint that no Blacks—King's peers—served on the jury was echoed throughout the bar.

"If it happened in Los Angeles, it should have been tried in Los Angeles," said Bertha Wilson of Compton.

Henry Graham, who runs the restaurant, said:

"King probably would have got a fairer trial by the Ku Klux Klan. Finding those officers innocent was like saying what Adolph Hitler did to the Jews was fair."

Rev. Jesse Jackson offered:

"Rodney King's civil rights were violated and the whole world was watching...The message sent from Los Angeles today will not stop at the California border. It will give aid and comfort to every racist in America.

This decision must be resisted, it must be actively and aggressively resisted with disciplined non-violence, or an already terrible situation could become even worse."

Retiring Los Angeles Police Chief Daryl F. Gates, provided this prospective:

"This is the time for us all to join together and say to the people of the City of Los Angeles, 'Let's keep it cool. Let's be civil to one another'....I think we have a system of justice. We've just witnessed that system work. We might not like it. We may disagree with it. That's our prerogative to do. But we ought to not prejudge the system."

Beloved Los Angeles Mayor Tom Bradley responds:

"I understand full well that we must give voice to our great frustration. I know that we must express our profound outrage, our anger. But we must do so in ways that bring honor to ourselves and our community. We must not bury the gains we have made in the rubble created by destructive behavior.

"I was shocked. I was outraged when I heard that

verdict. This jury told the world that what we all saw with our own eyes wasn't a crime. To acquit every officer on every count, in my wildest imagination, I could not have imagined, I believe that the issue of the justice system, based upon race is something that I would have to say was a factor. I cannot in any other way explain the jury's decision."

The lawyer of Rodney King, Steve Lerman, lamented the following:

"Any right-thinking normal person who sees that video tape and experiences the shock and viciousness of this event can't sit with this verdict as being the final say."

Statement of the 12 jurors and their alternates.

"This experience has been a very difficult and stressful one, one which we have agonized over a great deal. We feel we have done the best job we could have possibly done."

Officer Laurence Powell, acquitted officer, happily described:

"Very happy. It's hard to be surprised when you felt that way all the time. I know I'm innocent and that was the verdict."

The prosecutor in the case, Terry White, vents to say:

"I was shocked and disappointed. That's the way the system works. Apparently the jury had a different view of the videotape than we had."

Benjamin Hooks, executive director of the NAACP, aired his feelings:

"Bitter and the verdicts are a gross injustice, outrageous, a mockery of justice."

Heightened tempers, frustrated over the verdicts, became a volcano rage, the intensity of the hot ash translated into stores and business establishments being set ablaze by angry rioters during the evening following the not guilty verdicts. Anyone and everyone residing in or near South-Central California had to have frayed nerves, thinking and trying to imagine how far the burning would reach. Commonly put, 'Will I and my dwelling be spared?'

The Lakers played the Portland Trail Blazers that night at the Forum and were apprised of the nearby inferno. Security however, was definitely in play surrounding their locality and well-being.

Meanwhile, the beginning day on Wednesday, April 27, 1992, was very calm and ordinary. Pete was residing in his sister's condo in Culver City, California just behind The Fox Hills Mall. It was just the calm before the storm. Dr. Martin Luther King was indeed a modern-day prophet when coining the quote, "The threat of injustice anywhere is a threat to injustice everywhere." Of course, injustice was amplified and vocalized in that jury's not guilty verdicts which resulted in liquor stores and other establishments, going up in smoke immediately following the not guilty verdicts. Such riotous crowd assaulted non-Blacks, some critically. Bricks, rocks and other objects were thrown at individuals.

Poor Reginald Denny was pulled from his truck and was assaulted by an angry mob.

Just after telling Ray of the not guilty verdicts, he came over to Pete's residence. What nerves! They would sometimes work out together in the confines of Pete's residence, but not that particular day.

Pete worked at USC and to get to Pete's residence, if he didn't take the freeway, such travel would have to take him through the core of the turmoil and violence, but he arrived without incident.

"Let's go down the street to see what's going on?" Ray suggested. "Naw, Pete related facetiously. "Let's go," Pete replied.

Residing in Culver City, CA at the time, vandalism to establishments was sporadically scant. However, the owner of this Audio/Video store where Pete steam-cleaned its carpet periodically, wasn't spared but sustained minimal damage. The glass entrance door was broken out with shattered glass strewn mostly at the entrance of the store. The proprietor was of Chinese decent.

Ray whispered in Pete's ear, "Tell him you'll clean the carpet and extract the shattered glass as a good-will gesture."

Such kind gestures on Ray's part was what Pete saw initially in him to qualify the establishment, best friend. Obviously there were opinions to the contrary, some alleging arrogant, ill-tempered and sore-losers. The truest barometer of one's characteristic make-up is the consistence, measurement of time. Being their long-time softball coach and friend, such was translated to true qualifications of a leader; a leader who wasn't too receptive to another trying to impose his will or ways on him. Ill-tempered translated into a tenacious will to win, never yielding to losing until the lost is final. Sore-loser. Totally hog-wash. He can never be charged with not shaking the opposition's hand following a loss, even if the opposition was asinine. On the other hand, supposing an antagonist was asinine and initiated a physical challenge, it's on.

Time has somewhat mellowed Ray's temper as Pete recalled when some knuckle-head motorists in LA getting into a verbal altercation with him. There were about 3 individuals in a car yelling unpleasantries at Ray and as they came to a stop, one of the three pulled out a hand-gun, pointing it at Ray. "Does it take that to whip my behind?" Ray inquired. This period occurred in the late 80s or early 90s. Obviously Pete cautioned him to never do that again, being that some individuals have low opinions of themselves and disdain for the value of life itself.

Sometimes Ray, under certain circumstances, would give to the homeless and underprivileged. On one particular occasion, a disheveled-looking male asked him for alms. Ray gave him what he had available. The recipient responded, "That's all you gonna give me?" "It's more than you gave me," Ray retorted.

Fortunately, the burning, rioting and looting subsided as the National Guards were called in to quell the disturbance. Again, when gross injustice occurs anywhere it becomes contagious everywhere, as sporadic disturbances flared up in Atlanta, GA.

Buck, Pete's younger brother, was working in the metropolitan area of Atlanta, GA, and witnessed young Black males attacking Whites, punching and kicking, innocent individuals. Fortunately, while witnessing these beatings and walking away, he would meet two White couples walking towards where the beatings were occurring. He said, "Please don't go that way, my people are jumping on Whites there." "Thank you brother, thank you brother", they thankfully rendered and took a different direction.

It definitely was a sad and bleak period that soured race relations, putting a divide and dislike between Blacks and Whites. This aspect was strengthened and reflected as TV news broadcasters, referred to looters as savages, thugs, and hoodlums.

Immediate and sharp objections to such inexcusable name-calling by news broadcasters stopped. Rodney King's appeared on T.V. and pleaded, "Can't we all get along" did assuage some of the ongoing animosity, plus The Arsenio Hall Show was a platform to encourage peace and calm.

Pete's church was in South-Central Los Angeles, although he resided in Culver City California. One Sunday in May 1991, in his own perspectives, described related areas the appearance of a 'war zone.' The smell of smoke was very strong and smoldering continued to ascend the atmosphere. Black-Americans, living with the distasteful, not too-distance past inhumanity of injustice, presumably and inwardly declared, whenever injustice rears its ugly head against any of us, there should be a great response from all of us.

Eventually changes were caused in the wake of the upheaval, and time had its way of healing and *mollifying*.

But before time could soothe the turbulent memory of eventualities, Angelinos were shocked by the two grisly murders of O.J. Simpson's ex-wife, Nicole Simpson and her friend, Ronald Goldman. The murders occurred in Brentwood, CA, in 1994. Moreover, people were baffled over O.J. being charged with committing these hideous crimes. Conversations at work at the water cooler, the break-room and practically everywhere the question was: "Do you think he did it?"

Former Heisman Trophy winner from USC didn't seem to fit the profile of a double-murderer. Rather articulate and extremely personable — no, he couldn't be the killer. He appeared in movies, ran through airports as a pitchman for Hertz Rent-a-Car, and became a television sports commentator.

In 1969, he was the number one pick in the NFL draft of the Buffalo Bills. In 1973, Pete couldn't help but get chill-bumps and teary-eyed as he surpassed the season rushing mark, just past 2000 yards. "O.J. Simpson," he'd utter after that impressive run.

Months prior to these gruesome murders, O.J. was photographed in 1994 playing golf with President Clinton.

In the 1993, Thanksgiving Day NFL game, he was pictured on the sideline with wife Nicole.

Any measurement of success accorded to him in life, was given to his mother, who worked at San Francisco General Hospital, a psychiatric technician. He'd tell how his mother would not only steer his life on the right path, but helped his then, wayward friends.

Before O.J. Orenthal James Simpson, he was called "Juice." Anyone who saw him on the gridiron, faking and literally out-running would-be tacklers, (Juice was ideally befitting).

When comparing, he was always compared with Jim Brown greatness. Despite any contemporary running backs breaking Mr. Brown's all-time rushing record, Jim Brown was arguably the greatest running back ever. And for a short career, Gale Sayers was something special. But to Pete, O.J. was observed as the second greatest running back to Mr. Brown.

Not too many Angelinos can forget what they were doing during the Bronco Chase with Al Cowlings driving while O.J. held a gun to his head threatening suicide. Pete was glued to the TV watching the NBA finals. The 60 mile chase started in Orange County and lasted nearly three hours then ended when A.C. drove to O.J's then Brentwood Estate. As many individuals watched the unfolding news on TV, there were droves of people cheering him, because this was a very popular individual who was charged for an unpopular crime. People were eager to hear his side of the story. The drama of the Free Way Chase was the final episode the world had seen repeatedly in fictional flicks, only this thespian was all-too-real and unbelievable.

Many individuals watched on TV, whereas there were hordes of others lined alongside the Free-way with everything so surreal yelling and cheering "O.J., O.J," obviously had compound thoughts, this can't be happening and consequently, how will it play out.

That eventful evening wound up at O.J's Estate in Brentwood, CA. Mr. Simpson would be allowed to use the bathroom and ironically, was allowed to have a glass of orange juice. Subsequently, taken to Los Angeles County Jail, where he was booked, finger-printed, charged and jailed for the double homicide of his former wife and her friend.

At the time, Pete knew two individuals who worked at the County Jail, one would tell of always seeing Mr. Simpson. "What is his mood or facial expression?" Pete would inquire. "He acted calm and normal" was the reply of his friend.

Understandably, Mr. Simpson received an abundance of correspondences from family, relatives and well-wishers.

It was whispers around the Black-American community, that prosecutor Ms. Clark was despised, presumed out-to-get Mr. Simpson. Innocent or guilty, there was something about this case awakening the suspicion of consciousness of Black-Americans, preserving innocence until everything was on the table and consequently scrutinized.

Mr. Simpson's battery of attorneys were impressive, possessing razor sharp intellects and an acute knowledge of the law. Head attorney, Mr. Johnnie Cochran, wove his strategy point of attack and legal plan into a beautiful tapestry of effectiveness.

He initially clamored very loudly, the prosecuting team in the case was guilty in, rush-to-judgment. And in his assault of the evidence, stating vociferously it had been compromised due to cross contamination, citing such gathering was a cesspool of contamination. Additionally drawing suspicion on one of the key prosecutors' witnesses, Mr. Mark Fuhrman, the detective who allegedly scaled the wall of Mr. Simpson's home and consequently finding a blood-covered glove that was linked to the murders. He would later perjure himself when asked my Mr. F. Lee Bailey, attorney for the defense, had he used the 'n' word within the last ten years when addressing the member of the Black-American race? His "No" reply would later prove otherwise.

Then Detective Vanatter, through questioning by the defense attorney, would reveal that he carried a vial of O.J's blood that was voluntarily given by O.J. at the Parker Center after being booked. This procedure illuminated very brightly suspicious underhandedness.

After languishing in jail for nearly 16 months, Mr. Simpson was tried and acquitted on all counts of the double murders, sending shock waves of discontentment, disappointment and disapproval throughout the White community. Being more than aghast, the White community was infuriated and beside themselves. Just prior to the not guilty verdict, Mr. Cochran , who had been successful in a lawsuit brought against Signal Hill cops in Long Beach, CA of assault of a Black-American young man, was well familiar with rogue cops and then reminded the jury the impropriety on some cops behalf involving Black-Americans.

Adjoining, Ronald Goldman's father was outraged, saying, "That man, (Mr. Cochran) is sick, the police department isn't on trial, it's O.J. for killing Nicole and my son," he exclaimed. The family of O.J. would counter by saying "We didn't say anything when the prosecuting attorneys attacked O.J."

The prosecuting team perhaps caused irreparable damage to its case when they asked Mr. Simpson to try on that old glove confiscated behind his Estate, which clearly appeared too small for his hands.

"If it doesn't fit, you must acquit," said Mr. Cochran repeatedly.

In criminal charges, the prosecutor has the burden of proof beyond a reasonable doubt that a defendant committed a crime. A judge has the discretion to admonish a jury it has the discretion to acquit a defendant if there is reasonable doubt the accused didn't commit the crime for which he is charged/ and or if the prosecutor wasn't convincing enough during the presentation of its case to warrant a conviction.

Many Whites didn't like the idea that Black-Americans were celebrating the acquittal, feeling Mr. Simpson got away with the double murders. Though Pete was elated with the verdict, he did consider the victims and their families, thinking how badly they grieved the senseless and brutal knifing of Mrs. Simpson and Mr. Goldman. One had to inwardly ask, 'how would one feel if it happened to my kin, relatives or friends?'

Based on the evidence provided by the prosecuting team with the very possibility of cross contamination, and considering the conduct of some of the principals involved, certainly raised a very substantial reasonable doubt, making an acquittal conceivable and understandable.

On the following day, Oct. 4, 1995, while shopping in the California Mart, many Blacks wore facial glee, and Whites displayed stunned disbelief and notably disgusted expressions. One Black volunteered, speaking softly to Pete, "You should have been in this place yesterday, Whites were infuriated, extremely mad and upset over the verdict."

Undoubtedly, a cloud of glum and gall hung over many Whites, surmising and questioning the wheel of the legal system. Many of whom say the presented evidence against the accused overwhelmingly proved him guilty. Conversely, Black-Americans' perspective on the evidence — but compromised and fabricated. And the acquittal verdict vindicated their belief which caused the mood of exhilaration and jubilation.

Mr. Johnnie Cochran, defense attorney, the lead man in the trial of the century, accusing the prosecuting team regarding the crime scene and labortory a cesspool of contamination, during the aftermath, prompted an investigation into this accusation. A confidential review of department's Scientific Investigation Division obtained by The Times identifies 24 areas in which the laboratory needs improvement or needs to work with the research community to develop better crime-fighting techniques.

Some of the entries, which were prepared at an LAPD "technology summit held in the spring of 1994—before the murders of Nicole Brown Simpson and Ronald Lyle Goldman—point to significant problems in the lab's operations.

"The present system for replacing outdated or irreparable laboratory equipment to maintain analytical capabilities in the forensic laboratory is cumbersome, obsolete and inadequate," the report said. It identified a number of instruments that either were broken or in need of replacement.

The report also highlights an area that the Simpson team focused on, but which prosecutors contested. What the government lawyers did not say—and may not have known—is that LAPD officials privately shared some of the same doubts about the Police Department's DNA laboratory that the Simpson defense team raised.

In Fact, the report implicitly acknowledges that the LAPD's DNA technology does not meet minimum industry standards—much less the leadership role that the LAPD likes to claim for itself in American law enforcement.

"Scientific Investigation Division requires space, equipment and personnel to meet and exceed the minimum standards to perform analyses which would provide for complete and rapid identification and comparison of body fluids using DNA technology," the report said. "City management should acquire space, equipment and personnel to meet and exceed minimum standards for personal identification—as gas *vecine* standard in other criminalities laboratories throughout the country."

The revelation of recorded tapes of Mark Fuhrman that he and other officers committed misconduct during their tenure as officers, stoked increase suspicion of his character as truthfulness is called into question.

Consequently, the Police Commission and the department's Internal Affairs Division each launched investigations. Their missions: to determine whether Fuhrman was telling the truth when he described incidents of misconduct, and, if so, to figure out whether any new action can be taken by the department to address them.

Then Police Chief, Willie Williams publicly vowed a thorough review, but others in the LAPD were privately skeptical that much would not come of it. Many of the Fuhrman tapes were made nearly 10 years ago, and the incidents he describes are in some cases many years older than that.

"I don't think there's going to be much resolution," said one person familiar with the LAPD probe. "We'll end up with a ton of information, and there will be some embarrassments, but most of this is going to be out of statute, too old to prosecute and Fuhrman's gone, so what are we going to do to him?"

Fuhrman identified other officers in his taped interviews, suggesting that he collaborated with colleagues in some of his most notorious acts. Those officers now may face more trouble than Fuhrman. If the department could establish that they committed misconduct—and if those acts are not so old that they do not exceed the statute of limitations—suspensions, even dismissals—could be the action taken.

The trouble with that was that anyone accused by Furhman had a ready-made response: He is a proven liar.

"They'll say he's lying, and since we know he lies, that's pretty hard to argue with," one LAPD source said.

Apart from the narrow focus on Furhman's allegations, the department also has pledged a renewed attack on racism in the ranks.

Pete, from his carpet clientele, knew a client who didn't only know Mr. Furhman, but once employed the former embattled cop, saying he was a tough guy who used to work in the Rampart district.

The provided particulars present more than reasonable doubt pertaining to acquittal. Everyone found guilty of a crime is not guilty. Conversely, everyone acquitted isn't innocent. But the greatest amount of those accused usually end up with guilty verdicts. Black-Americans usually being on the losing end—and when the acquittal verdicts swung Mr. Simpson's way—celebratory joy was inevitable. The prevailing consensus by some Black-Americans at the time was, irregardless of innocent or guilt, maybe this case was one slipping through the cracks or compensatory to so many atrocities and heinous murders committed in the past by Whites against Blacks.

One thing for sure, it polarized Americans and left an acrimonious taste in the minds of many with fall-outs that continue to linger today. After all about 3 years removed from the LA riot following the acquittal of those cops in the Rodney King's fiasco, venting in the form of rioting, placed a racial divide in race relations.

Despite having come a long way with an immense improvement in race relations, there was prejudice among us at the sociological and economical levels. Even President Bush, in a speech recently advocating more Black-Americans should be given the opportunity to own homes and businesses, realizing that there has been disproportionately and prejudicially denied access to loans from which their counterparts have benefited and enjoyed life.

Pete' remembered a white realtor friend related reading old documents which explicitly read..."Don't grant loans to

Blacks and Hispanics." Her response was, "I was appalled," she lamented. Pete's perspective on racism reads, "What is racial prejudice or racism but a gangrene plagued individual who is mentally overwhelmed with rubbish and cancer until eventually and inevitably it will consume that individual."

Meanwhile, race relations can become more harmonized and viable once we begin to love our neighbor as we love ourselves, Biblically speaking. We change the world in which we live when we make a change within ourselves; replacing prejudice with patience toward everyone. Patience recognizes the need to eliminate prejudging based on appearance, it shows kindness and meekness whenever bitterness and inauspiciousness are dealt. Quite simple, don't respond in kind.

Hatred should be replaced with humility; humility embraces understanding. Understanding is a prudent teacher that all forms of haughtiness is figuratively, a malignant cancer that gradually eats away character until the whole person is eventually consumed. Wherefore life bears witness that many adults today are not grown-up psychologically; but, are immersed in stupidity and ignorance...

Before the trial of the century, came the announcement of Mr. Simpson being charged with double-murder. From the beginning, many just couldn't come to believe he committed these gruesome murders. But there were those who initially held the predilection to the contrary. Attorney Johnnie Cochran warned everyone about prejudging, including the prosecutor's 'rush to judgment.' Sure, as a caring and sympathizing society we moan and groan for justice, realizing what happened to Mrs. Nicole Brown Simpson and Ronald Goldman wasn't fair at all, wanting the assailant or assailants brought to justice. As previously asserted: no one gets away with murder..."Judge not, for we all one day will be judged," including the person or persons who savagely caused those deaths. There is a "Higher Authority" who will exact judgment on all His mundane creatures, especially towards those who annihilated so many jews and Blacks in the past. What is racial prejudice or racism but a gangrene plagued mentality or an individual so overwhelmed with rubbish and cancer until eventually it will consume the whole?" Blacks and Jews, were observed as sub-humans. That same Higher Order is the One who tapped President Abraham Lincoln with sensitivity and discernment to declare the Emancipation Proclamation in 1863, which was eventually enacted in 1865. He saw something special in Black's character and DNA make-up, who once exclaimed, "One could take 150 Black men and defeat a whole continent of people."

God has really blessed America, which is by far, the greatest country in the world. It's inhabitants shouldn't be too consumed with revenge when considering in the future, judgment that awaits everyone by God.

The atrocity of injustice done to minorities in the past can never be undone, but as a special people, exercising poise, patience and resolve, with such faith, Blacks will emerge a stronger people, physically, emotionally and psychologically.

When spanning a lifetime, the greatest challenging trauma to befall Pete was the loss of his mother, Fannie, in February 1999. He once described it as if someone had just literally snatched his heart out...and that life stood still and nothing again would ever be the same. Since she smoked cigarettes, and in an attempt to get her to stop smoking, he once told her that if anything ever happened to her that he would check out also. Just prior to her death while hospitalized she reflected upon his very words, and concernly questioned, "I don't know how that child (Pete) is gonna make it in California?"

Since Sally, Pete's sister, would always oversee her, it was Sally who should have been given the most attention, care and concern by supporting family members. Just after their mother's passing, Pete would send for her from Atlanta, GA to LA to help out in his carpet cleaning/general cleaning business, to keep her mind occupied. His often exhortation: "Stay busy, preoccupation is an effective substitution to sad reflection...remember, time might not heal pain but it certainly will alleviate it."

Meanwhile, he would continue his softball play, along with performing carpet duties, keeping busy.

Seven months following the passing of his mother, following a typical day which included activity and travel, he arrived at his pinay's house. And while sitting at the kitchen table, eating a meal she had prepared, such routine was anything, but routine. After serving his food, his pinay friend retired to bed.

While eating and nodding at the kitchen table, he inexplicably fell into a deep sleep. Somehow he envisioned walking through a narrow corridor and began to stumble and eventually falling literally while sleep-walking, hitting his head on either the kitchen table or chairs. The thud awoke his friend, sending her scurrying to find Pete on the floor semi-conscious and assisting him to his feet. "My neck hurts, call Ray," who would come there within a short time. After he arrived Pete insisted that she call Sally in Atlanta, GA. Sally would advise Ray and pinay on what to do and to call paramedics.

While at the hospital, x-ray showed a dislocation of the fourth and fifth vertebrae, whereby some sort of head and neck apparatus was put in place to re-fit the dislocation. After lying on his back for nearly 2 weeks, the aforementioned vertebrae were re-fitted to their normal positions, but a team of neuro-surgeons conferred, deciding to operate to stabilize his neck.

Such down time caused Ray and Andre to strategize about how to keep Pete's business going while he recuperated. Meanwhile Sally flew to California immediately to be with Pete to offer helpful information to doctors, who would team up with Ray's former girlfriend who was a pathologist. Ironically, the chief of staff knew Sally from Atlanta, GA, assuring her that he would put together his elite neuro-surgeons to perform the surgery. And ironically, would offer Sally a job since she was a swell RN.

Lying on his back nearly 2 weeks, to him it felt like an eternity. He felt helpless but having tremendous resolve and an enormous faith in God, fortified with family, sister and friends, accelerated his recovery time. Similar to a performer winning a Grammy and trying to thank everyone—that befits Pete's posture of appreciation trying to recall and thank everyone who played a part in his speedy recovery. Obviously God is number One, his immediate family; pina friend, Ray, Andre, Peggy, Dan, Dale, Spencer, the realtor friend, Diane, Ray's ex-girlfriend, Nancy, the pathologist. Greater Friendship Baptist Church in Decatur, GA, Ebenezer Baptist Church in Atlanta, GA, Mt Tabor Baptist Church in Los Angeles, CA. Pete offers a great, big hearty thanks to you and everyone involved.

Unforgettably while recovering following each day of work, his softball teammates and other would visit, milling around the hospital bed. "Dan, please tell everyone about the story of the Jehovah Witnesses?" Pete asked smilingly. With reluctance he started expounding the story. One day while washing his car in his yard, he felt eyes staring at him when these two individuals came up to him and started telling him about eternal life and Heaven. After listening intently and attentively, he looked the two straight into their eyes and offered, "Look, I got this nice house, car and a lovely wife and daughter, Heaven can't get any better than this." Laughter immediately filled the room.

Encapsulating the furtherance of race relations and lending a helping hand in a worthy cause, Pete shares an article he composed entitled Signs of the Time.

Hurricane Katrina's fury to the Gulf Coast has certainly left America and other conscious-driven Countries in a state of shock and bewilderment.

Finger-pointing has already begun, suggesting Government reacting too slowly, plus apathy and even racism on the part of the President is asserted. All of which could be the case, but what America should be doing is praying to God to bless those surviving individuals in Alabama, Mississippi and New Orleans, and at the same time, please make some type of contribution to the relief effort to aid those affected. After all, when a great misfortune befalls any of us there should be a great response by all of us.

Undoubtedly, God has really blessed America with wealth and prosperity and a willingness to come to the aid of other Countries during the time of emergencies. The latest catastrophe by Hurricane Katrina will likely go down in history as being the worst calamity America has ever experienced. And from this experience, it is extremely imperative that everyone, especially Americans come together prayerfully and patiently to trust God to guide us through this misfortunate event. Analogically, God is a giant Spool and people are the thread representatives, and each time we are on the same accord, mobilizing and praying collectively, we affect the Spool.

It is high time that everyone exercise repentance and acceptance of Jesus Christ now, stepping out of the shadow of darkness and into the sun-lit glory of eternal life of happiness.

That if thou shalt confess with thy mouth the Lord Jesus, and shalt believe in thine heart that God hath raised Him from the dead those shall be save. For with the heart man believeth into righteousness; and with the mouth *confession is made unto salvation." Romans, Chapter 10, Verse 9 and 10. Chapter 13 goes on to clarify, "For whosoever shall call upon the name of the Lord shall be saved."*

Meanwhile, let's continue to live harmonious and prayerful in order to keep the Spool moving in our favor. Additionally, you should love the Lord with all your heart and all thy might; and love your neighbor as oneself. To truly do this, we do well by placing our lives on the track of righteousness. It has been observed: To be in sync and alignment with the universe in being in harmony with God.

Basking always in God's love, peace and mercy.

Prayerfully,
Pete

Despite history not being very kind to people of color and the reprehensible nature of past generations of individuals, forward, we must move. The adage is loud and clear that... To overlook the past we usually are condemned to repeat it. Sure there are today, among us, seeds of the Devil, but by and large, we're coming together like never before. We are mending differences and thriving harmoniously. Realistically, to stare too long at yesterday, we lose focus on tomorrow, and while racing with the current, time usually runs out.

Twelve

Trailblazers

When scanning the horizon following the accomplishment of anything, Pete, didn't have to grapple at all where credit lies, it goes directly to God. Most importantly, he's given infinite thanks for life and the ability to perform mundane chores. And, when individuals omit God and begin rambling, bumbling, and babbling to include mundane creatures, and not the Creator, such verbiage becomes annulled, as do such individuals.

Significantly, we thank and praise God for calling upon His own number in Jesus Christ who paved the way for all to receive eternal life.

St. John Chapter 1, Verse 12 reads; 'But as many as received Him, to them He gave the right to become children of God" even to them that believe on Him name."

Recalling the evening just prior to neck surgery, Pete was given papers to sign authorizing surgery, September 1999. "Doctor, give me the up-side and down-side of the particular surgery?" Pete candidly inquired. "Well, the doctor who will perform the surgery has done this type

of surgery many times in the past with remarkable success."
Then he gave a preview of the procedures involving surgery,
then proceeded to say, "With the degree of difficulty regarding this type of surgery, there is a chance that you could die
during the procedure or you could sustain some form of paralysis," he reasoned. "Give me the papers, let's do it." Pete
exclaimed.

All that night Pete would hum, "There's Power in the Blood
of the Lamb." Sally visited him very early the subsequent
morning just prior to surgery, remarking, "You look very
happy this morning." Undoubtedly, he was enthusiastically
filled with spiritual optimism as everything during surgery
went flawless, the recovery, was just a two-month period.

Hence, he offers tremendous thanks to God for overseeing
the surgery, realizing, routine doesn't guarantee an unevent-
ful outcome.

During his two months period of recuperation, thanks,
and appreciation, are given to Ray, Andre, Don, Dale, and
those who directly made it possible for his business to continue while incapacitated.

Moreover, he praises his mother and father for shaping,
and molding his life into what it has become—a conceptual
composite, representing Christian character, and an over-
ready willingness to help others.

During adolescence, he would say to Fannie, "Mama, I'm
not going to say an Easter speech at church, I'm too old." She
would emphatically demand, "You're going to do something,
you must be going to sing; or maybe you're going to preach,
or perhaps you are going to say a prayer, but you're going to
do something."

There were principles she instilled in all six of her children; namely attending church, believing in God, and aspir-
ing to a higher education and responsibility. When any one of

us would say, "Mom, I'm not going to school today, I don't feel well." Such assertion would be met with her vociferously saying, "You might not go to school, but you're going away from here."

She had to abort her education in order to help out domestically. Of all of her seven sisters, she unquestionably demonstrated to be the brightest regarding intellect and responsibility of overseeing her sisters even the one who was her senior.

And for those who thought they knew her and those who didn't … she was a visionary and undisputedly had a direct connection with God, so much so, it was frightening. Pete, in his eulogy writing during the funeral, narrated the time when their father and his friend, Bussy, elected to drive from Chicago, Ill to Atlanta, GA, opposed to their usual train ride.

Awakening from sleep in hysteria, waking others, saying clearly something had happened to their father. Ironically, the same time she awoke was identical in time when his friend and driver had fallen asleep at the steering wheel as the car veered off the road with the car coming to a stop, resting precariously on a cliff. Had the car gone over the cliff, death to their father and Bussy would have been inevitable.

Clearly, God had given her a vision of the incident. The book of James is clear, "Draw nigh to God, and He will draw nigh to you." Fannie was unquestionably close to God and a visionary. The Kid, the oldest of three brothers, once forebodingly related a family member, "You know, sometimes when telling mother where I was going, and she'd say, 'Don't go there,' and I'd go anyway, something bad usually happens."

Pete remembers all too well the time she tried to take his car keys away, admonishing, "You should be coming in rather than going out," a formidable, agonizing odyssey.

Because of her relationship with God, and her love for Haymon, her husband, it is believed that she personally introduced him to God. Haymon was a cosmopolitan individual, affording him to develop an acute intuition and observation in dealing with circumstances and individuals. His job, a truck builder, at the Pullman Company, would take him from Atlanta, Ga., to St. Louis and eventually to Chicago, Illinois, working on segments of trains, particularly the wheel section. He loved his job and became well known, as an outstanding welder.

As a toddler, Pete recalls vividly when his father would come and leave on the train. It would sadden Pete to see him leave at the train station. On a particular occasion, standing with Fannie and the Kid, his older brother, hearing the voice of the train conductor calling out, "All Aboard!" The older brother, Kid, showed much emotion as he watched his father leaving. His leaving touched a sensitive cord in everyone with the Kid saying, "I wouldn't go back there (Chicago) for Mono Lisa's daughter."

After working 33 years at the Pullman Company, he would sustain a mild stroke, which forced him to retire, in 1966.

Being a champion of good character, respect, and decency, he took pride in his attire, fashioning tailored suits all of his life, complemented with owning and driving mostly Buicks. When attending an event, what Fannie called, "Balls," included dancing and mingling, he never would dance but would stand and talk, showcasing suits fit for a prince and squire. Women would huddle and say, "I could have a heart-attack over him." Then you could hear one say, "That's that woman husband." Fannie was an extremely beautiful woman as Haymon arrayed her also with fine clothing. This is a clear explanation why Buck, the youngest of three of his sons, is mentioned to-date, being the best dressed male ever to grace God's world, thanks to a design skill, extrapolating conceptual visuals from the 30s and 40s, gleaning pointers from his father's uniqueness and from avid study of those eras.

Haymon, who indeed was deemed a cosmopolitan man, moreover, a rather wise man, thanks to experience and his keen observation. Whether his six children asked his opinion or not, he just the same provided it regarding the company they entertained. Similarly to a prophet, he admonished his oldest daughter, Ethel's, boyfriend, saying, "If you don't straighten up your life, you will be in jail within six months." That prediction came to fruition about four months later when he robbed a jewelry store, wielding a gun, demanding, "If you want to live to see Christmas, then hand it over!" Yes, he was busted.

Of all the guys who would come to their house to see Pete, he provided opinions on everyone, and ironically, the two whom he liked, became Pete's best friends, namely Charles and John.

To-date, Charles who was reared by very reputable and fine parents, church-going, and decent individuals, influenced his life into the right direction. He didn't only join the church, but he is currently serving as an usher and has become a positive symbol and image.

John, who was a classic mama's boy, life has translated into a tower of success and impressiveness. Being a mama's boy isn't bad and can be good and does not project a sissy image, depending on the mental make-up, resolve and perspective of the mother. Mrs. Augustine is a very strong and intellectual lady, modeling an image of independence, grace, and perseverance. She's complemented with a neat husband, Mr. Ralph Augustine, a quiet but unassuming man whose life illuminates respect, decency and optimism.

The culmination of John's life can be credited to both his parents, but it is Pete's perspective that Mrs. Augustine is the main militating force behind his accomplishments. Admittedly, during a period when Pete didn't exercise or maximize sheer observation and intellectual might is recalled while visiting John on a particular Sunday following attending church service. Mrs. Augustine inquired, "What did the preacher talk about?" With a blank stare and milling over thought, Pete stuttered and rambled to say little to nothing, which brought forth much laughter on all behalf. Mrs. Augustine was a Jehovah Witness.

Pete recalls a particular occasion when Mrs. Augustine broke the ice, that John had bought rings for his then-girlfriend and would be marrying shortly. "Did you hear about your boy who's engaged and getting ready to marry?" Such announcement brought on paralyzing shock to Pete in that he'd keep such gigantic news from him; his ace friend. She would show off the purchased rings. The lady to whom he was engaged, on that proverbial scale of 1 to 10, registered 12. Ironically, that potential engagement never materialized, as he later confided, "Despite her looks, she was an air-head."

To-date, thanks to God and positive-driving parents, his entrepreneurial skills have propelled him into a successful businessman in the Atlanta area. Besides, being the proprietor of several businesses in the area, something he and Pete did on occasions, has been taken to astronomical heights — fishing. He is considered to be perhaps the first Black-American to host his own fishing program. Angler's Paradise can be seen on the Black Family Channel in Los Angeles every Saturday evening at 9:00 p.m. His knowledge of fishing is crystal clear, which matches also his exuberance, making him a natural.

While visiting Pete in California in 1987, John was accompanied with his son and daughter, John-John and Carolyn. At that juncture he confided, "I finally attained one of my aspirations." Pete, non-surprisingly responded, "I knew you would,"

Psychologically, in an attempt to steer John-John properly, he inquired. "Pete," tell John-John most of the things we did while growing up," Pete stated. "Unlike many of the young guys today, our biggest fun was fishing, working on cars and dating lots of young ladies ... We didn't steal, rob, or hurt anyone, we didn't mess with drugs, but had natural fun doing those things mentioned ... but we'd drink beer occasionally."

If ever, one wanted to see a wide vivacious smile on either Pete's or John's face, ask either to name one single place where they had the most fun? The exclamation point would read: "Peyton Place!"

A lesson to teens: Choose wisely your friends, examine their ways, characteristics and ambitions, they largely should reflect yours. Anyone who doesn't reflect what you stand for, immediately desist association.

The dark era of yesterday is inevitably entrenched in memory but should never rest on one's mind adversely since we know now an all-sovereign Creator will, during the final analysis, preside over and reckon with the dockets of everyone. His creation, particularly individuals, should continue to live out their purpose in life, being of help and serving others in a patient and positive posture, which brings a smile to God's face. Never mind about prating and senseless discussions concerning the derivativeness of life, we all came from God; nor being that concerned about the destiny of life, we shall all return to God, bracketed between life and death, we should be a loving service to humanity.

The living Word (The Holy Bible) is on point when it reads: "The fear of the Lord is the beginning of wisdom, and to depart from evil is understanding." While no one knows the perfect order of the Almighty's minds, but being his kindred via Jesus Christ, qualifies one to safely surmise He doesn't rest in the bosom of foolishness, impatience, and ungodliness, but delights in the understanding of the wise.

Black-Americans shouldn't be over-wrought over the fall-out of Michael Richard's tirade, when Black hecklers verbalized he wasn't funny. Infuriated perhaps by his own inability to incite funny jokes, he took a journey back into memory lane, implying, fifty years ago we'd have you upside down with a F___g fork up your ass." He then said repeatedly, "He's a...N."

Immediately following his outburst, he apologized to the hecklers and to all Black-Americans.

Such tirade shouldn't be charged to this man's heart; rather, his head. Most importantly, it speaks volumes of past dehumanizing acts against Black-Americans, which illuminates very brightly in memories and minds today. Matter-of-factly, everything a person says does not exit in the heart, but the continual display of a person's action, judges the heart.

A racist, Mr. Richard is not; a funny comedian, he's not, which fueled his frustration leading to his racist tirade.

The use of the 'N' word is something Richard Pryor said he'd stop using during the latter part of his career. Despite making an extreme amount of money, making people laugh using the word, when it became a reproach of conscience, it became a taboo to Mr. Pryor. When Black-Americans use the 'N' word, it is a comedy and mode of communication and is not necessarily wrong. But if such usage convicts one, then refrain from its use. The Hip-Hop generation uses it as hip and something as being cool, enunciating it: "Nigga".

Pete's girlfriend who was a bit slow comprehending a lot of the western language, asked Pete what does the word nigger mean?   He would explain, "Historically Whites would refer to Black-Americans as niggers, which means low class, no-good people. But that description could be labeled on any nationality being that no one is any better than anyone; instead, we are who we are because of choice, and whatever we've become, we've chosen to be that."

In 1989, his girlfriend Nita, needed tires for her car and would follow Pete to this tire place in Hawthorne, CA. Pete lived then in Hawthorne, about ¼ of a mile from the tire company. He had to return home for some reason, telling her that he would be right back. Returning home there was a voice mail message on his phone from his friend which was upsetting in tone.

Returning quickly to the tire company, finding Nita extremely irritable, and when asked what was wrong, she angrily points at the White male in charge, and said that he was waiting on customers who came in after her, charging, "He's a nee-ga." With his mouth wide open, deer-in-the-headlights eyes, the shaken man tried to explain to Pete that some customers came in for different things besides tires.

It took every ounce of strength in Pete's body to keep from laughing as he tried to console her. Of course, he cautioned her to never call anyone the 'N' word again.

There is much validity in the axiom there's a place and time for all things. Depending on who uses the 'N' word and how it is being used should be an exception and not the rule. Though Pete cautioned his pinay friend to never used the 'N' word again because the way she used it was injurious and character-attacking. Blacks have been hurling the 'N' word around like it was a frisbee toward each other with no ill intent almost forever. Plus the hip-hop culture have revolutionized the word by putting an 'a' at the end, in their lexicon, means tough, cool and happening. And since rap and hip-hop are growing, the lyrics are etched in the mentality and into contemporary society. However, such acceptance of the word should be given careful review.

REMEMBERING ROSA PARKS 1913 - 2005

SOME CALLED HER the precipitator of the Civil Rights movements, where she was known also as the mother of the C.R.M. This strong, courageous individual passed away October 24, 2005, at the age of 92.

Her home going was graciously celebrated by dignitaries and lay-individuals, and remembered practically by everyone, especially by the U.S., knowing she was a person who changed the course of history by refusing to give up her bus seat to a White passenger in 1955.

To magnify and construe what she did in 1955 was nothing short of heroism in that she risked physical harm and liberty, when inwardly she presumably said, "Enough is enough. I'm tried of this blatant inhumanity and injustice, even if it causes going to jail or being beaten." The Jim Crow rule was nebulous clouds that hung over Black Americans at the time—and certainly a distasteful reminder—the servitude of slavery wasn't quite a hundred years old and that the more things change the more they stay the same.

The Emancipation Proclamation, was issued by President Abraham Lincoln, January 1, 1863, but due to a sin-sick mentality, Blacks were disdained and perhaps deemed sub-humans by the mere practice of separation and inequality. Many Black-Americans living today can recall the White only signs reserved exclusively for White individuals.

It would be sad commentary to list or cite the number of Blacks who were killed, and some lynched just because of the color of their skin. A very good friend of Pete's, in his book, "Don't Call Me Preacher," who happens to be White, tells how a grieving widow came to him crying and wanting to know why this Black man was acquitted in front of eye witnesses for killing her husband, who also was Black. Approaching the then Prosecutor/Solicitor General to ask why this happened. His poignant response was, "Well, to them, (an all white jury) it was just one "N" killing another "N." This situation occurred in Georgia, the latter part of the sixties.

This White pastor tried to make a difference by clinging to his principles; protesting alongside Blacks in Georgia, when inequality and injustice reared its ugly head. During a particular protest, someone in a crowd yelled at him, "You can't do that, it's against the law!" "Yeah, but there are laws that's wrong," he shouted back.

Whenever any law is out of harmony with the balance of justice, fairness and impartiality, one has a moral right to challenge it. Thanks to Mrs. Parks, she exercised a challenge many dared to undertake — demonstrating civil disobedience paved the way to changing a law of bigotry and racism — whereby today Black-Americans enjoy an immense measurement of freedom. Oprah Winfrey acknowledging today it was Mrs. Parks who allowed her the opportunity to be where she is today. Sport athletes are extremely thankful to her for opening the money vaults to be paid salaries not only exceeding that of the President of the United States, but making it pale in comparison. Despite the quiet inequity of the movie industry, the Denzel Washington(s) and Halle Berry(s) can thank Mrs. Parks for her temerity, refusing to get up so today people of color could be comfortably seated in a litany of opportunities enjoyed today. Thanks to this legendary pioneer for unlocking the shackles of the concept, "If a person isn't given an opportunity to fail, then it is impossible for that person to succeed."

This former seamstress' refusal to relinquish her seat to a White male passenger that Thursday, winter of 1955, galvanized a nation and changed a reluctant 26 year old minister named Martin Luther King, Jr., who became the greatest civil rights leader in history.

For her act of defiance, Mrs. Parks, 42 at the time, was arrested, convicted of violating a segregation law, and fined $10, plus $4 in court fees. Consequently, Blacks in Montgomery boycotted the busses for nearly 13 months while mounting a successful Supreme Court challenge to the Jim Crow law that enforced their second-class status on the public bus system.

Just a year prior to the bus incident, May of 1954, the Supreme Court handed down the historic, Brown vs. Board of Education, decision banning segregation in public schools, interestingly, Mrs. Parks was an activist in the south helping to enforce the law of the land.

The Montgomery NAACP, spearheaded by activist E.D. Nixon's strategies, had desired to challenge the racist public transportation laws there, meaning Parks' case was considered divine intervention.

Born Rosa Louise McCauley, recalls the nights she lay on the floor next to her grandfather who sat in a rocking chair armed with a shotgun over ready to challenge Klansmen who were terrorizing his community.

She reflected upon many a day she'd walk to a segregated school in Pine Level. All the White children would throw trash at her and her classmates from their bus as they rode by.

Parks' credited her grandfather with instilling in her rebellious passion for fairness and equality; saying, "You don't put up with bad treatment from anybody." It was passed down almost in our genes.

Her father, James McCauley, was a free-lance carpenter and builder who traveled regularly, and her mother, Leona McCauley was a schoolteacher. Parks was two years older than her brother Sylvester.

Mrs. Parks was awarded many honorary medals. Among them, the two highest civilian honors — The Presidential Medal of Freedom, and The Congressional Medal of freedom. President Bill Clinton, who awarded her the Presidential Medal, said, "I was honored to award her the Presidential Medal of Freedom. She was an inspiration to me and to all who work for the day when we will be one America,"

In remembering Mrs. Parks, we dare not overlook the "Man", attributing much accolades and accentuation to the ultimate drum major for justice and fairness. Dr. Martin Luther King, Jr., 26 at the time of the bus incidence, was pastor of the Dexter Avenue Baptist Church in Montgomery, who was drafted to lead the Montgomery Improvement Association, the organization formed to direct the nascent civil rights movement.

Though, he was drafted by earthlings into the civil rights movement, simultaneously, he was highly favored and chosen by God to implement his life's role that was fulfilled so daringly and admirably.

The Montgomery Improvement Association formed a Transportation committee that established a virtual transportation system for some 30,000 daily boycotters comprised of private cars and station wagons.

February 1956, Dr. King and other ministers of the MIA members were indicted on charges of violating Montgomery's boycotting law. Parks was re-indicted. King was found guilty, but the case was appealed.

Refraining from riding busses for twelve or so months must have involved pain of inconvenience, legging out many miles per day just to get to jobs and businesses presumably was physically taxing. Many jobs Black-Americans would lose, but what was gained in the aftermath was the elimination of bigotry and racism while riding public buses. What contemporaries enjoy and take for granted today, was paved by forerunners who sacrifices will always be remembered and appreciated. Retrospectively, Black-Americans can affirm, "The highest enjoyment of attainment is the recognition of effort and sacrifice."

During the civil rights movement, there were many who paid the ultimate sacrifice, whereas today one can hear whispers of young males naming athletes their heroes. The lexicon of listing the word hero should be tucked so far away in a nook and never, ever extracted or alluded to unless it merits the mention and affixed on the likes of those civil individuals and armed servicemen and women, especially those who knowingly and willingly submitted to the ultimate sacrifice. Those are true martyrs and heroes. If the intellect begs the question, "What about those individuals emanating from exotic areas of the globe, strapping explosives to themselves in the name of their God, detonating and killing themselves and scores of little children and other innocent people?" Heroes? An emphatic not! Rather, these crazed, hell-bound idiots are carrying out wishes of another demonic and deranged individual or individuals. Present Bush calls them evildoers.

There is this reputable pastor and fine tooled theologian who graces the TV screen and vehemently stresses regarding The Holy Bible. "If you don't get the beginning right, one certainly won't end up getting the end right." While receiving an innumerable amount of letters from viewers with assorted questions pertaining to the Bible and contemporary events, one viewer wrote wanting to know what will happen to the evil-doers of "9-11" when facing God. All living souls (people) when departing this mundane life will go to a gulf, a detaining dimension in the presence of God, and will remain there until the millennium. This erudite theologian offers matter-of-factly, "I hope they're wearing some asbestoses proof drawers when facing Him (God)."

Ruefully, in many cases, the truest significance of a cause isn't totally appreciated and realized until it has been encapsulated by time. Appreciation is infinitely given to the likes of Mrs. Parks and those who paid the ultimate sacrifice, especially to Dr. Martin Luther King, Jr., who too was an erudite, God called person; someone to whom all people can appreciate and emulate. A bona fide hero.

Rev. Jesse Jackson, said of Mrs. Parks, "She sat down in order that we might stand up ... Paradoxically, her imprisonment opened the doors for our long journey to freedom."

The drum major for justice and arguably perhaps the best orator since Jesus Christ in his writing, "Stride Towards Freedom," Dr. Martin Luther King, Jr., wrote, "Actually no one can understand the action of Mrs. Parks unless he realizes that eventually the cup of endurance runs over, and the human personality cries out—I can't take it no longer!" Mrs. Parks' refusal to move back was her intrepid affirmation that she had had enough. It was an individual expression of a timeless longing for human dignity and freedom. She was not planted there by her personal sense of dignity and self-respect. She was anchored to that seat by the accumulated indignities of days gone by and the boundless aspirations of generations yet unborn."

CHRONOLOGICAL PERSPECTIVE OF
CORETTA SCOTT-KING

AT THIS WRITING, it's unfortunate commentary to report, January 30, 2006, Coretta Scott-King passed away. She was stricken by a heart attack and stroke in September 2005. Mrs. King was an extraordinary lady who not only mirrored much of the philosophies of her husband, but was perhaps the conveyor of some of the perspectives articulated by him. Whenever their home was bombed, how many of us, male or female, would have stayed the course? Perhaps most would have said, "I have only one life and to escape this (the bombing), I'm changing my course of living." Rather, she didn't only stay the course, but joined her husband in further demonstrations and thus was known as the first lady of the civil rights movement. She was the living embodiment most women presumably emulated and adored. She set out to be a singer, but became known as a symbol of beauty, class, grace, and intellect.

Pete's sister, Sally, is a member of her church, Ebenezer Baptist Church, in Atlanta, Georgia, the church as which Mrs. King's father-in-law preached, (Daddy King). Also, the church at which her husband would preach many sermons. And needlessly mention a place of worship where a crazed gunman would end the mundane life of her mother-in-law, Dr. King's mother, during the early 70's. In short, Ebenezer Baptist Church is a legendary landmark and shrine whereby to-date is perhaps the number one choice frequented by tourists visiting Atlanta. Most importantly, viewing the crypt of Martin Luther King, Jr., that sits eastward adjacent the church amid a water fountain, a sacred place at which many come and toss coin pieces into the fountain and just reflect back into time, thinking had such not occurred, what would it be like regarding the development of today.

Since Coretta Scott-King once said she wanted one day to be buried alongside her husband, it is understood at this writing accommodations are underway.

Meanwhile, her funeral and home-going was fit for a queen, and was attended by a myriad of celebrities and dignitaries and exceeded in length, her illustrious husband's, which lasted some five hours. From the Whitehouse, February 3, 2006, President Bush wrote:

"Our nation is deeply saddened by the death of Coretta Scott-King. Mrs. King was a beloved, graceful, and courageous woman

who called America to its founding ideals and carried on a noble dream. She was a great civil rights leader, and her contributions to freedom and equality made America a better and more compassionate nation. The United States of America is grateful for the good life of Coretta Scott-King."

Laura and I were honored to have known Mrs. King, and we will always treasure this one   thing Mrs. Coretta Scott-King once said, "I learned that when you are willing to make sacrifices for a great cause, you will never be alone, because you will have divine companionship and the support of people. This same faith and cosmic companionship sustained me after my husband was assassinated, and gave me the strength to make my contributions to carrying forward his unfinished work."

On behalf of the people of Atlanta, while we mourn with you now, we know that you will find peace in the memory of her lifetime commitment and contributions to carrying out Dr. King's unfinished work."

Sincerely,
Shirley Franklin

There were so many positive remarks by so many individuals during the eulogy of Mrs. King, from Joseph Lowery, former President Jimmy Carter, to former President Bill Clinton. Former President Jimmy Carter talked about the mean surveillance of J. Edgar Hoover of the King's family, and particularly M.L.K. Junior.

Those individuals who weren't at the funeral sat in stoneface solemn watching on T.V., absolving eulogy after eulogy of praiseworthy remarks from President George Bush to former President Bill Clinton. Always a crowd favorite and someone who's very adapt at working an audience, but more so, besides his dolce elocution — delivers deep thoughts. With his hands gesturing to the casket, verbalizing, "This was a beautiful lady who never lost her beauty ... She was a role model, try modeling the life she lived."

Pete's sister heads the Welcoming Committee at Ebenezer, and when she isn't greeting on Sundays, she schedules others (church members) to do the greetings. Sally does a wonderful job addressing an audience and appears a natural at it, exhibiting clarity, style and charm.

Pete recalls fondly the 100th birthday anniversary of Daddy King that was held and conducted in the Historic Ebenezer Baptist church where Daddy King and son, MLK Jr. delivered many a sermon. It was beautifully choreographed, using video and audio of interesting dialogues Daddy King had with family, friends and church members, covering everything from ethnicity to racism. Pete even helped pass out the programs. In attendance was Ethel, Pete's oldest sister who's in education. Coretta asked Sally who was Ethel since the two resemble in appearance. She would also introduce Pete to Mrs. King.

At the conclusion of the ceremony, Pete mustered up enough courage to speak to Mrs. King, narrating the time when her husband was on a flight with this White woman to, it was believed, Washington, when the woman blurted out, "I wouldn't want my daughter to marry one." After a few moments of silence, Dr. King shouted back, "I wouldn't want my daughter to marry George Wallace, that is, if she was old enough to." ... Exclaiming further, "You're expressing an unconscious racism — what is racism but the assertion that one race is inferior to another and that God made a creative error?" Noticeably, tears had begun to well up in Coretta's eyes.

ENCAPSULATING THE MAIN TRAILBLAZER

DUE TO A fast moving world, many a time one might not realize the truest significance of a cause, purpose or individual until they have been encapsulated in time. Dr. Martin Luther King, Jr., was Pete's mentor, but sadly, didn't realize his truest significance until later in life. The history books are inaccurate describing MLK, Jr., falling immeasurably short delineating who he was, what he represented and his overall significance. The MAN himself once asserted after departing from his earthly life to not look at any academics he may have amassed, accolades such as winning the Nobel Peace Price, where he matriculated; rather, offering, "Know that in the end, I tried to help somebody."

That's exactly what he was doing during his last mission trying to help those boycotting sanitation workers, when a lone assassin, perhaps with the backing of conspirators, ended his mundane life. God's handprints were smeared all over this man's life and accomplishments as he lived assuredly and undauntedly toward life's purpose. His remarks following the assassination of John F. Kennedy, were naturally sadness and shock, but prophesied matter-of-factly, "The same thing is going to happen to me."

The amplified question is: How many of us, specifically red-blooded Americans, would do what this great man did? He once said, "If there isn't a cause or person so dear to you that you wouldn't give up your life for, then you're not fit to live." When promoting a cause, endeavoring to implement a purpose where the treat of death loomed ubiquitously, many, if not most individuals would jump ship. Having a direct line of communication with God, he presumptuously vowed, "This cause is much bigger than man, if God permits man to kill the temper, my soul, he has no control … In fact, there

is no weapon formed against me shall prosper." Affirming
he had been to the mountaintop—that his eyes had seen the
coming and the glory of the Lord—like previous prophets
and God's elect, recognizing when God is for you, who can
be against you? Though you may slay me, yet will I live, he
inner affirmed and resolved.

Yes, we agree mundane contemporaries elected him to be
their leader during the civil rights movement, but he was officially installed by God to lead it. One woman said immediately after he was elected to lead the civil rights movement, that,
she wasn't impressed by a mere Baptist preacher leading the
bus boycott, but there was something special about him. (Dr.
Martin Luther King, Jr.). Another male exclaimed, "There's
no doubt this man is a leader." These reflections were noted
at the very beginning of his election, but now and beyond
history, etched in the annuals of recordings and spirituality,
his time shared among us was directed and guided by the
auspices of God, and God alone.

It would be foolish and senseless to equate any mortal ever
lived to Jesus Christ, who was God-man incarnated. It evokes
similarity to Darwin attempting to explain away evolution,
despite intense study theorizing findings "though not conclusive but very striking nevertheless," he quoted.

It doesn't require a magnifying glass to interpret the conceptual purpose that Dr. King promoted and endeavored to
implement. It was unmistakably Jesus Christ. The same power that spoke the planetary objects into being, created man
and woman and calling upon His own number, fashioning
and clothing oneself in flesh to become the perpetuator and
substitute for humanity's sin. Abolishing the out-dated blood
sacrifice of animals for the atonement of sins, and became
the ultimate sacrifice and escape route from death to eternal
life. This Grace and Love were merits we didn't deserve but

a favor from God many accept and relish henceforth. Essentially, during Christ thirty-three years among mortals, His main message to a wayward world was to repent and to be redeemed. Christ was a beacon for humility, humbleness and non-violence. The word of God is spiritual nourishment and our life map, pointing out, "The fear of God is the beginning of wisdom, and to depart from evil is understanding."

It was customary that each year, Mary, the mother of Jesus, and husband Joseph, would travel from Galilee, City of Nazareth to Jerusalem to the feast, but on this occasion, bringing along the twelve year old Jesus Christ, their son. The imaginary throng of people traveling to and at the feast, must have been tremendous, while walking from the feast, Jesus lagged behind and ventured into the temple. When Mary and Joseph looked around for Jesus, he was nowhere to be found. After back tracking from where they had traveled, their three day search would find him in the temple teaching to doctors and presumably dignitaries, as they were confounded by his wisdom and understanding. It was believed Anna, the prophetess, the daughter of Phanuel the tribe of Aser, was at the temple absorbing the wisdom the twelve year old was imparting as individuals started to mill around. Biblical statistical recordings suggested after marring and having lived with her husband some seven years before becoming intimate; moreover, she (Anna) was on fire for the Lord who served him with fasting and prayers night and day, addressing everyone about God's great redemption.

But for Jesus, one could hear whispers of amazement: "Is that Joseph's son imparting profound wisdom at such tender age?"

Even his mother, Mary, was amazed at this manner of wisdom and elocution, inquiring, "Son, why hast thou thus dealt with us?"

The replying Jesus offered: "How is it that ye sought me? Wist ye not that I must be about my Father's business?"

That is, He knew beforehand his life's mission — working in collusion with the father — His poise, patience and persistence to undertake a mammoth challenge in which only God could succeed. Even John the Baptist lauded the Savior saying, "There would come one who's mightier than he whose shoes he wasn't worthy enough to unloose. Pointedly revealing, "I indeed baptize with water, He shall baptize you with the Holy Spirit and with fire." Luke, chapter 3:16.

And when John the Baptist did baptize Jesus, from heaven, an audible voice of God immediately proclaimed, "This is my beloved son of whom I am well pleased."

The Savior of the world is incomparable is every facet, form and findings, and is the world's ultimate paradigm and paragon from whom all should emulate. Attempting to do so, Dr. Martin Luther King, Jr.'s life is called to mind as a modern-day notable with scintillating mentions. Similar to God calling upon His own number to save the world from perdition, It would be safe and sage to say He tapped Dr. King to implement a purpose.

While no one can measure, gauge or estimate any one person's personal relationship with the Lord, each merits its own experience. Dr. King was usually accompanied by close associates, friends and supporters, but, it was obvious this fine trailblazer shared quality and quiet time with the Lord. But for him, on several occasions, to surmise someone someday would kill him; acquainted him with the notion, percentages are, the establishment or prediction of a person's future foreshadows one's contemporary lifestyle. Conversely, known between he and God was a marvelous revelation preview of circumstances to come. And to say he'd been to the mountaintop whose eyes had seen the coming and glory of God, was confirmation of that glorification. God gave him a revelation and preview of things happening then and things to come. This revelation has to be likened to the occasion when Jesus took Peter, John and James up into a mountain to pray as Jesus' garment became as white as show, and began to glister, plus His countenance changed. Luke, chapter 9:29-31. Sleepiness affected Peter, John and James during Jesus' prayer to God, but when awakening, it was clear and unmistakable what they saw. Consequently, Peter's unsteady voice inquired to Jesus, "Jesus, Master, is it good for us to be here: and let us make three tabernacles; one for thee, and one for Moses, and one for Elias: not knowing what he was saying. While He spoke a cloud overshadowed them, as they became fearful as the voice of God could be heard saying, "This is my beloved Son, hear Him." Luke, chapter 9:31-35.

During the revelation preview, there is no telling what God allowed Dr. King to see. But for sure, he was shown something. Black-Americans have endured affliction, degradation, dehumanization and even death during recent history, with Dr. King leading the way to promote their freedom; freedom from deprivation of equal opportunity, justice and equality. During these endeavors, God was certainly and actively in the midst and center of things as they were unfolding.

With firsthand experience, Pete and Sally's revelation, seeing that Shepherd during their childhood days was real and not an illusion and will always be remembered. The all sovereign God does reveal some revelations to certain individuals for reasons in many cases, very discernable. It was unmistakable in this case God cares for all life, even little innocent birds, and didn't want Pete to kill them senselessly. Moreover, He knew one day Pete would share what he saw to a stiff-neck, hard-to-believe world. Sally asked her brother, "Why did God want me to see that Shepherd, I wasn't killing birds?" "Quite simple, to Him, in time, it was just a moment ago, meaning, He knew what you were going to do by helping elders ... Playing Santa Claus, distributing gifts to the elders in the community in which you were born; when taxes were raised, you, with the aide of God, appealed to the proper source, getting them lowered. Look what you do for the elders who are members of Ebenezer Baptist Church, who are unable to attend church, residing in assisted living homes, how you bring them home cooked meals. Just this past Christmas 2007, you took a home cooked meal to Mrs. Rice, who is blind. Yes, God knew of your kind heart during its very nascent or before you knew it. With the help of God, think of your success in getting two streets renamed in honor of two significant individuals who once lived in the community."

Meanwhile, during the exodus, Moses led the Israelites from Egypt through the Red Sea and wilderness, on display luminously, was God's sovereignty, mercy and might. The same source was with Dr. King during the turbulent 50's and 60's, lending a long arm to the civil rights movement. Perhaps from God, King was shown and/or in the midst of pantheon of prophets and elects who preceded him during the implementation of God's divine scheme.

Black-Americans were perhaps observed by God as the modern-day Israelites, a race of people who were held captive, and yearned naturally for freedom, equality and justice. The Almighty enjoys the right to show favor to whomever he will, and especially the oppressed and victimized. Like Dr. King's predecessors who were chosen by God, he too was called by God to lead the freedom march for Black-Americans who were initially kidnapped, scourged, many killed, and forced into abject captivity of servitude.

The trumpeter once exclaimed, "When any law is out of harmony with God's law, man has a right to break that law."

The civil disobedience through protests revolutionized muta-tion whereby Blacks and the poor today enjoy its fruits, but the price tag was extremely high which translated into mar-tyrdom, thanks to the drum major for justice and other civil rights advocates.

It has seemingly taken an ion for society to start treating Blacks equitably and fairly. Memory and awareness are very fresh in the consciousness of society today regarding their mistreatment to improving treatment. But, to draw a line in the sand in comparison to the Jewish race, and sleuth history, the similarity is striking.

Also striking in similarity was Jesus' short earthly life to that of King's abbreviated life. Biblical accounts of Jesus' life were 33 years, and Dr. King was 39 years old when departing this earthly life.

Jesus, God incarnated, taught in the temple at twelve years of age; and King skipped the 9th and 12th grades of school, graduating from high school at sixteen, and today, is regarded perhaps the best orator since our Lord, Jesus Christ, and was unquestionably endowed by God with profound intellectual-ity and spirituality.

Conclusion

This story is a true account of my life. I've always wanted my parents to know my deep-seated appreciation of them, particularly their sacrifice and work ethic, and all the time they spent to raise their six children. Additionally, I thank them for their advice, especially their spiritual advice, which has molded my character into the person I am today.

My writing was inspired by the blatant racism I've encountered, which taught me the importance of developing character without losing my dignity. I have seen some of my brethren who have suffered the indignity of racism which has adversely altered their lives. I've worked alongside someone who charged, "I hate all White people and don't like any Blacks who like White people." A lifelong frustration regarding the past mistreatment of Blacks by Whites leaves a psychological scar, causing some individuals to hate, use drugs, and turn to a life of crime to vent. Obviously, that's bad and does not lead to a wholesome character. There are many non-Blacks who dislike Blacks with a similar passion.

I believe a person dies daily who claims to hate his fellow man, simply because it takes energy to hate. It has been theorized that strong anxiety produces some forms of stomach ulcers. Probably racial prejudice and racism lead to cancer because the mind is certainly diseased.

I liken racial prejudice, or racism, to gangrene, because it plagues and rots the individual until mentally, he becomes so overwhelmed with rubbish that it overflows his body physically with cancer, which eventually consumes him.

Though I was very young at the time, the scene at that ice cream parlor started my curiosity to churn, causing me to question the very fiber of this great country. How can I forget the time when Sally and I had to ride the bus from school to our house just before I purchased my first automobile? We didn't know the bus fare had increased when we went to deposit the money while exiting. Somehow, Sally had sufficient fare as she placed her coins into the slot. "Naw, you can't get off until you pay your full fare," the grim-faced White male driver informed me. Fortunately, a kindhearted Black lady asked me how much I needed, and she paid the difference.

The assassination of John F. Kennedy deeply disturbed me, and it left thoughts tumbling in my mind. Why would anyone want to assassinate or murder another person? Even more troubling was the distasteful events that frequently occurred during the civil rights movement, when people were simply pursuing equality, equal rights, fairness, and justice. Many Black and White lives were snuffed out by what Dr. Martin Luther King Jr. described as "our sin-sick White brothers."

I can still hear my sin-sick supervisor at Sears say that Dr. King was nothing more than a troublemaker. I can still see the breaking news on TV during that time that showed police dogs attacking Blacks, with high-power water hoses smashing blacks, policemen knocking Blacks to their knees and hitting their backs during civil rights protests spearheaded by Dr. King.

Even though prejudice and racism still exist and impact our country, today, thanks to those individuals who paid the ultimate sacrifice during the civil rights era, we enjoy major progress in the opportunities now available to us.

Prior to the publication of this book, democratic contender Senator Barack Obama had not yet announced his candidacy for the presidency of the United States. Mrs. Hillary Rodham Clinton was still mulling the idea of her candidacy. I figured if she ran, she would surely get my vote. Admittedly, either candidate would be a welcome and sorely needed replacement for the present occupant of the highest office.

It is people like Rosa Parks, Dr. King Jr., and others who paved the way for this grand opportunity of a Black-American man and a White woman posturing to become the commander-in-chief of our nation. Surely Dr. King is leaning at the portal of those pearly gates with a broad smile on his face thinking that his sacrifice wasn't in vain.

I would like to close, reminding my readers to sacrifice themselves lovingly and help others, particularly the destitute, the widows, the disabled, and those who can't help themselves. Let hastiness be replaced with patience, poise, and persistence.

God reminds us in His Word to be anxious for nothing. Don't become overly concerned over the origin of life, for we all came from God. Don't be overly concerned about the destiny of life, for we all shall return to God. Live your life in such a way that you can lovingly serve all humanity.

Most importantly, never harbor revenge. Remember, revenge does not foster a pristine image; rather, it clones the characteristics of evil, which in the end, leads to damnation.